THE OT

FALKLANDS

The Lion and the Lamb

By R. M. Edwards

Typeset by Howden Press Services,
233, Albert Road,
Southsea, Hampshire,
PO4 OJR

Printed in Great Britain for
DRIFT PUBLICATIONS,
82, Drift Road,
Clanfield, Waterlooville,
Hampshire, PO8 ONX
by Apex Print Services,
Hillside Industrial Estate.
Horndean, PO8 OBL

The Other Side of The Falklands
by
R.M.Edwards

ISBN 0 9522041 0 X

THE OTHER SIDE OF THE FALKLANDS

The Lion and the Lamb

THIS BOOK IS DEDICATED TO THE PEOPLE OF THE
FALKLAND ISLANDS WHO PROVIDED THE MATERIAL FOR
THE MEMORIES

My thanks are due to Pat Lee for the cover design and the pen sketches, Michelle Rossiter for her patience in proof reading, and friends and colleagues who provided help and encouragement.

Although the names of some people have been changed where considered appropriate, all the incidents in this book are true.

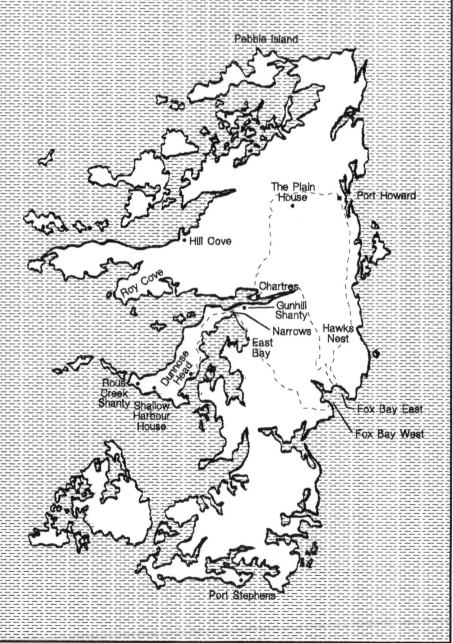

The West Falklands

Pebble Island

The Plain House

Port Howard

Hill Cove

Roy Cove

Chartres

Gunhill Shanty

Narrows

Hawks Nest

East Bay

Dunnose Head

Rous Creek

Shanty Shallow Harbour House

Fox Bay East

Fox Bay West

Port Stephens

CONTENTS

CHAPTER 1

THE FALKLANDS AND THE HANNE S

If first impressions are lasting, then anticipation must contribute to the memorable effect that the first sight of the Falklands and of Stanley must have on the majority of people who arrive at the islands by sea.

First light on a somewhat misty March morning saw the *Hanne S* approach the entrance to Port William that led on into Stanley Harbour. The Cape Pembroke lighthouse spelt out its warning that we were approaching land after a four-day relatively uneventful voyage from Montevideo. Uneventful can mean many things but to any boat or ship in the South Atlantic it must include the absence of stormy and gale-lashed seas.

The dark outline of the islands emerged to reveal the narrow steep-sided entrance to the harbour that seemed no more than a stone's throw from one side to the other.

The early morning mist had cleared by the time we entered Stanley Harbour to reveal the town in the watery sun. Five or six rows of white painted houses with the occasional red or green painted roofs, dotted at random throughout the town, which rose, gently at first and then rather more steeply, to stop short of the jagged ridge that dominated the skyline. The Cathedral church, dedicated to Christ, with its whalebone arch standing strong and yet enveloped on three sides by the closely congregated houses, seemed to herald the warmth, help and support that the islanders had to offer and were invariably willing to give.

As we edged closer, the harbour scene became alive. The Falkland Island Company jetty was surrounded at its head by the rugged and jaunty hulks of steam and sailing ships of decades past. Ships smashed by the inhospitable seas around Cape Horn, spared long enough to limp into the safety of the islands, only to end their days as provision stores, Custom sheds and workshops.

Further along the harbour, close to the Town Hall, Post Office and Government House, was the less imposing public jetty. In the harbour, anchored and acting as if it was a giant weather vane, was the *SS Fennia*, its sailing days over yet still afloat and serving as a timber store.

Stanley had two guest houses, one hotel, four pubs, two clubs and six stores. It had been arranged that I would stay at the guest house owned and managed by Mrs Carrie McLeod, a warm congenial lady, whose house on Drury Street above the green leading up from the Post Office, was home to about six men. They included two who lived permanently with her and worked in the town, three members of a survey team, who spent their time between Stanley and the icebound Dependency bases of the Antarctic, travelling to and fro on the Royal Research Ship *John Biscoe*, and Harry Sarnie,"a camper", the name given to those who lived and worked on the outlying sheep stations, Harry was spending a few weeks in town, on holiday.

The roads, which were poorly maintained, totalled less than twenty miles, including a five mile stretch to the lighthouse at Cape Pembroke. Stanley radio station broadcast to the sheep stations, known as the camp, for just a few hours each day, with many of its programmes relayed from the BBC Overseas Service. Within the town, a public address system operated through loudspeakers in each home, playing music, giving public information, local news and advertising newly-arrived goods in local stores.

It soon became apparent that the United Kingdom was home to all Falkland Islanders and, although many of them had never been there, they talked with knowledge and affection of their ancestral home.

Preparations for me to go to the islands from the United Kingdom had been arranged at breathtaking speed since I had spotted a small advertisement in the *Portsmouth Evening News*: **"Wanted young men to work on sheep farms in the Falkland Islands"**. It went on to invite those interested to apply to an address just half a mile away from my home in a small country village in Hampshire. Within minutes I was on my bicycle determined to find out more, there were many questions to be answered, such as where were the Falkland Islands and other small details of similar inconsequence.

I was a few months past my twentieth birthday. My grandparents on both sides of the family were from farming stock and even while still at school all my weekends and holidays were spent on the farm cleaning out the pigs and cows or driving horses during the harvest time. Admittedly I knew nothing about sheep, other than they had two ends, one of which ate grass, but that was no barrier. As I was to learn later, the majority of young men who found themselves treading the same path had been brought up in towns and cities of southern England and had no experience of farm life at all.

My parents were very unhappy with the prospect of me going so far away from home. For me the fact that it was so far away, a mere eight thousand miles, made it all the more exciting and worthwhile, after all anyone could go to America or Canada, but it seemed that very few people had been to the Falklands and far fewer knew where they were.

In four short weeks my application had been accepted, a passport issued, and Tuesday 16th February 1954 nominated as departure day. I learnt from the agent who had placed the advertisement that there was another young man, Albert Hatch, living in the next village, who would be travelling on the same ship. Albert was a year or two older than myself, but it soon became clear we had one thing in common and that was neither of us had any idea what lay over the horizon. Had we experienced a change of heart and mind, our general education and worldly experience would have lacked both colour and substance.

Our ship was the 500 ton cargo vessel *Hanne S*, registered in Copenhagen, with a Danish crew. She was bound for the Falklands with a general cargo and nine passengers, leaving from dock number ten in the port of Southampton, which was conveniently only a few miles from home. The excitement and anticipation of the future did little to mask the wrench of saying goodbye to our families. My father drove Albert and I to the docks where we met up with the other seven passengers, who, like ourselves, were leaving home for the first time, with the exception of Willy MacBeth and George Douglas, the latter preferring to be called Geordie. Both were Scots and returning to the Falklands for a second term of contract and from whom we were going to learn a little about the Falklands and a lot about life.

Loading the ship took a lot longer than anticipated and in the intervening forty-eight hours before finally leaving, we busied ourselves settling into our cabins and the routine of life afloat. What at first looked like a large ship, was in fact a very small, cold damp and sometimes wet tin can. The main accommodation consisted of two double cabins below the bridge and close to the engine room. They were well presented and warm, but very noisy and the air was filled with the pungent smell of diesel fumes.

The remaining cabins were in a hastily partitioned forecastle, the entrance to which was down a vertical ladder, secured to the bulkhead.

Three cabins were on the port side of the forecastle, while on the starboard side was the paint store, the ship's maintenance material. Right forward, and some ten feet from the foremost cabin, were the anchor chains and the haws-pipe through which the chains passed before being secured to the two anchors, just a few feet from the cabin when the anchors were winched tight to the bow.

We were to learn that expressions like 'plain sailing' and 'a bed of roses' had no place on this ship. The crew, of whom there were 15 in all, spoke little English, but sufficient for those occasions when the message, rather than the spoken word needed to be communicated. The food was typically Scandinavian, cold processed meats and raw pickled herrings, which were kept in the paint locker alongside the paint, paint brushes and oily rags.

The Solent was shrouded in low cloud and fine rain was falling when shortly after mid-day on Thursday 18th February a Trinity House pilot cutter came alongside to take off the pilot who had brought us out through Southampton Water to a position just east of the Isle of Wight and from there we were on our own. First stop Las Palmas, second stop Montevideo and then Stanley, but before we could contemplate stepping onto dry land again there was one experience hitherto unknown to most of us, but both notorious and well known to experienced sailors, the Bay of Biscay.

There was nothing by way of entertainment to distract our attention from the marked deterioration in the weather and in consequence the swelling sea outside. A ship the size of the *Hanne S*, barely forty feet wide, needed no encouragement to roll and pitch. The gangways on either side of the cargo holds were filled with forty gallon drums of diesel oil and lashed to the top of the holds were a number of cars and vans, all destined for the colony. Shipping costs were calculated by volume, hence the Captain's desire for cars on the deck, passengers in the forecastle and oil drums in the walkways around the deck.

By early evening it became apparent that all was not well with the human cargo, the overpowering smell of oil-based paint, rope and pickled fish that circulated in the forward section added up to just one thing. No way was I going to allow myself to be shut behind and below that forecastle door, until we had settled into calmer waters and that was still some days away.

For three nights and two days our small sea-going island was tossed and twisted by the merciless sea of the Atlantic Ocean. The waves were higher than the bridge, the ship shuddered from stem to stern as it rose on a mountainous wave before plummeting back down into the seemingly bottomless trough that sent a wall of water crashing over the bow. When the ship lifted and fell one anchor swung out from its supposedly secured position, only to come crashing back with a force and fury likened to an exploding cannon as its vibrations resounded throughout the length and breadth of the ship.

The brief time that I spent in my bunk was a little short of a nightmare, bracing myself for the low climb out of a trough, feeling the shudder as the propeller came unusually close to the surface, only to plunge back down into the depths. I spent those memorable nights in the mess, wedged as best I could in a corner seat, sleeping for a few minutes at a time as tiredness overtook me.

After two days the Captain, concerned about the non-appearance of many of his passengers, instructed the steward to bring them out of the cabins to sample the delights of the fresh air and, hopefully, to have something to eat, while attempts were made by the crew to clean up the cabins. So violent was the weather that ropes were strung the length of the deck for us to support ourselves, lest we should be swept overboard. Even then we were instructed to wait until the deck had been floodlit from the bridge and we were climbing out of a trough, before attempting to travel across the deck.

By the fourth day life seemed to take on a measure of reality. We were well through the Bay of Biscay, the sea was calmer and the temperature some ten to fifteen degrees higher than that which we had left behind in Southampton.

Boredom was beginning to take a grip of us all by the time we reached Las Palmas in the Canary Islands on the seventh day. Spells of homesickness had swept over us all at some time or another during the journey which reduced us to a miserable group of despondent travellers on being told that our stay was to be a mere three hours, sufficient only to take on fresh water and fruit.

It was 7 p.m. by the time we came alongside and already dark. The lights of the docks and the city beyond were an open invitation for our first run ashore, although the instruction from the First Engineer was clear. "We leave at ten o'clock tonight, be here, or we leave without you."

A few minutes later nine conveniently deaf passengers climbed into two taxis which were standing on the dockside waiting for just such an opportunity. "Where you go", was the question put to us. "Where you take us" was the united reply. Off we went, glad to be on dry land, even if it was to be short-lived, twisting and turning through the streets of Las Palmas until after a few minutes we stopped sharply outside an imposing building with wide wooden doors. We tumbled out of our taxi and in through the door like travellers from the desert who had just heard that beer was about to be cancelled. There was beer all right, although the price was five times that which we had been accustomed to paying back home, but it was probably due to the high wages paid to the staff. There were rather a lot of them. A further unusual feature was that they were all on our side of the bar. Clearly the house was of a somewhat unsavoury nature.

We downed our most welcome, even if expensive, ice cold beer and left as hurriedly as we had arrived. So it went on, a few drinks here and a few there, some friendly bartering with the ever present street traders, until it was time for us, with marked reluctance and much misgiving, to return to the ship. Somewhere along the way we had lost the second taxi and with it about half of our fellow travellers.

The Captain was showing signs of anxiety by the time we arrived back on board, pacing back and forth between the Bridge and the gangway, anxious to be underway. Fuel, water and other stores had been safely embarked and the ship was ready to leave, without passengers if necessary.

Having exhausted his knowledge of the English language trying to elicit information from those of us who had returned by the due time, the Captain instructed the First Officer and the Bosun to take a taxi and go looking for our wayward shipmates. The possibility of having to look for the proverbial needle in a haystack paid off, either by luck or the experience of veteran sailors, conditioned by first hand participation in a run ashore, they found their quarry after just a few minutes, making their way back to where the ship was berthed, on foot, caring little whether the *Hanne S* had left without them or not. The Captain's English improved greatly as he gave them a dressing down, to little effect. Remorse was not one of the new experiences acquired ashore that night. The boys having drank copiously from the cup that cheers, were all well past caring for the Captain's wellbeing. It was nearly 2 a.m. when we left the dockside in

Las Palmas. So intent were we on securing the presence of our shipmates that we had failed to notice that our cabins in the forecastle had been host to an unwelcome visitor, during our brief stop. Total inexperience had allowed us to ignore the possibility of an opportunist thief taking advantage of an open porthole. An ably assisted, very thin, light-fingered Spaniard had made off with one of our most prized possessions, the source of all our entertainment, a gramophone, thoughtfully leaving behind just one damaged record.

The days grew longer and warmer as we travelled further south. The crew erected an improvised swimming pool by suspending a canvas tarpaulin between the ship's derricks and filled it with sea water. It made a welcome change from just sitting on the sun drenched deck; the magazines and paperbacks had all been read a dozen times.

The only immediate thing to look forward to was the next meal, the passage of time and the monotonous routine of inactivity, had even made that look attractive. Respite came from time to time, when, without warning, flying fish leapt clear of the water and landed on the deck. The Bosun spent much of his leisure time preserving the larger ones for use as table ornaments.

The day before we crossed the Equator dawned with a new dimension to our understanding of the fickle nature of the sea. It was as if we were floating on a piece of glass, so smooth was the water that even the boat cutting through it failed to cause a ripple on the surface. It seemed totally uncharacteristic, quiet and still, stretching as far as the eye could see.

At precisely 3.20 on the afternoon of March 3rd and sixteen days after we had said goodbye to our families in England, we crossed the Equator, our exact position recorded as latitude zero zero zero degrees and longitude twenty-two degrees. The Captain in the guise of King Neptune assisted by his Queen, Davy Jones and the Royal Babe, held court to pass judgement on the 'Polliwogs', the name given to those, whether they be passenger or crew, who had never crossed the line before, so that they be well and truly initiated into the Ancient Order of Shellbacks. It was a wet, messy but colourful occasion which called for all participants to be lathered, shorn and dunked into Neptune's Royal bath. The celebrations went on well into the night and by Royal decree we were each allowed to have one bottle of Carlsberg lager.

Our next and only other stop before reaching Stanley was still many days off. The fresh fruit taken on board at Las Palmas, but for a few oranges, had disappeared, and we were left with the all-too-familiar processed meat and cheese.

The lack of variety and quantity became a focal point which gradually made us more and more dissatisfied each day. It was usual for the crew to eat first, in the tiny mess that both groups shared. It was at tea time on one particular day that a difference of opinion on how the passengers should be fed, or more to the point, with what, came to a head.

The crew had already eaten when we went into the mess. Lucky for them bad luck for us, there was barely any food left, nothing on which to feed nine young men, ravishingly hungry and fully charged with boredom and frustration, all the food, safely gathered in, amounted to little more than six broken slices of bread, nothing else, bread, in numerous pieces. The last straw had fallen into place.

Our complaint resulted in the cook, who was also the steward, throwing his hands up in the air and launching into a torrent of unintelligible language, which neither helped to dispel our own feelings or our determination to solicit a more varied and wholesome meal.

On such a crucial issue the Captain had to be consulted, the consensus of opinion being that we had to take our complaint to the top. As the issue was one that affected us all, a delegation was required to present the case, not wishing to be accused of being the empty barrel that made the most noise, I suggested some ground rules, to demonstrate the strength of our feelings and was promptly elected to high office, on the premise that he who makes the most noise, leads the way. I set off up the steel stairway to the bridge, dutifully followed, at a discreet distance, by an apprehensive entourage. My speech mentally prepared, I knocked on the door to the Bridge, which was opened by a junior officer and asked to speak to the Captain, an awesome responsibility rested on the shoulders of one so young.

I began to wonder if I had done the right thing, maybe it would have been better to have accepted hunger as a condition of man and face it bravely. But I was there at the door of the Bridge, and the task in hand called for a calm but forceful presentation.

While I waited for the Captain to appear, one question kept coming to the forefront of my mind, was I really ready for the task? The Captain listened carefully as I explained the problems that had been mounting for some days and had now culminated in us being asked to sustain ourselves on a mere six slices of bread, and they, I went on to say, "Gave all the appearance of having been struck by lightning". A fatal mistake on my part. It was at that point that the funny side of the picture that I had just painted for him emerged, I began to laugh mid-way through the delivery of my complaint, which had the immediate effect of removing all seriousness from the subject as everyone, including the Captain followed my lead and crumbled into a fit of uncontrollable laughter. However all was not lost, on the contrary, quite the reverse. It transpired that the oil-fired ovens had broken down and the cook had been unable to make any fresh bread. The confrontation that had earlier ensued brought to a head our grievances. From that moment the food provided for us started to take on an appearance of that which we were accustomed to and personal relationships improved greatly.

The first indications that we were nearing land came when gulls were seen flying around the ship, a welcome sight and sound over the rhythmic throb of the ship's engines. Early the next morning the Bosun called us from our cabins to see a lone flashing beacon on the horizon.

Montevideo, situated on the eastern side of the Rio de la Plata, or the River Plate, less than 100 miles from the Argentinian capital of Buenos Aires, is the capital of Uruguay, a neutral country during the hostilities of two world wars. Possibly that same beacon, standing tall on a long man-made breaker which protected much of the harbour from the sea, that had guided the Captain of the ill-fated German battleship, the *Graf Spee*, to seek protection from the smaller ships of the British Navy, following one of the earliest battles of the second world war.

The Captain of our ship, remembering all too vividly what had happened the last time we had been turned loose on an unsuspecting public, made it clear that this time, although we were staying for seven hours, when the time came for him to leave, he was going, safe in the knowledge that Montevideo was a regular port of call for most ships on their way to the Falklands. One of these was the *R M S Fitzroy*, owned by the Falkland Island Company and contracted by the Government to make regular voyages to collect mail, passengers and other essential supplies and transport them the 1,200 miles to the Colony.

Being on a fixed term contract, we were entitled to be paid from the date that we had joined the ship in Southampton, which created the need for our first call to be at the offices of the Falkland Island Company's local agents, McLean and Stapleton. To each of us was handed, almost as eagerly as we were prepared to accept it, what was in effect nearly one month's pay, such had been the duration of our voyage thus far.

Montevideo was a beautiful city. Its wide tree-lined streets, flower-filled squares and beautiful parks, quite rightly earned it the title of The City of Roses. It was an enjoyable break, marred only by its brevity, although still sufficient to enjoy the hospitality which, not surprisingly, centred around the bars and open-air cafes.

Earlier in the day before going ashore, I had watched with nail-biting excitement, the antics of a little man, clearly making a living by his cunning and wit. A ship similar in size to our own was in the process of unloading bananas, great bunches still secured to their centre stalk, each one weighing as much as any man would wish to carry. Our little friend had somehow got into the docks and had seized the opportunity, seemingly when no one was watching, to remove for his own benefit and satisfaction a goodly supply of the forbidden fruit and was, as I watched, in the process of making his way out of the docks and into the city.

His progress was hampered by two smartly dressed, armed, policemen who somehow had detected his presence and he theirs, turning the encounter into an adult game of hide and seek.

Judging by the little man's nimble movement and his skilfulness at evading his would-be captors, this was a common occurrence, and by all appearances, successful, because while walking through the poorer parts of the city later in the morning, boys were quite openly offering small bunches of bananas for sale to the rather more affluent passers-by.

It was difficult to equate our experiences of the previous weeks with what we had been led to expect in the Falklands. There had been plenty of opportunities for Willy MacBeth and Geordie Douglas to give us graphic examples of their own experiences and the sort of conditions in which we could expect to find ourselves working, but somehow it did not quite fit.

This was the last leg of our journey, and yet here we were, in a busy city, the street cafes and the local bars helped to forget early frustrations, the people were friendly and the weather very warm. How could we be so close to the Falklands, if the winds were as hostile as we were led to believe.

This time all the ship's passengers were on board by the time the crew had made her ready to sail. For the passengers, the run ashore had possibly been more relaxing than we had imagined, when in conversation with the Captain the next morning the suggestion was made that we had all returned quietly the previous evening and dutifully went straight to our cabins, to which he swiftly retorted, in very understandable English, "Like hell you did, you were all fast asleep on the deck at three o'clock in the morning". That was four hours after we had left Montevideo, which could only be attributed to a brisk walk in the evening sunshine.

SEVEN HAMPSHIREMEN SAIL FROM SOTON TO ADVENTURE

"Echo" Staff Reporter

THE sturdy old British settlers, thousands of whom set sail from Southampton in little ships to establish the far-flung outposts of the British Empire, would have smiled approvingly today had they stood with me on the Town Quay.

They would have admired the handsome 500 tons Danish freighter, Hanne S, as she sailed into the drizzle of the Docks on the first stage of her 10,000 miles voyage to the Falkland Islands. Their pride would have been reserved for the passengers—nine young men who have signed contracts to work as sheep farmers for five years in the remote, sparsely-populated hills of the Western Isle of the Falkland Islands.

Seven of them have said goodbye to their relatives and sweethearts in the south-west corner of Hampshire where they were born and taught their craft. The other two, who only came back from the Falkland Islands after a term of five years as shepherds six months ago, have again left behind the land of heather and bagpipes to work in the Far South.

For the Hampshiremen, none of whom have been overseas before, this adventure and prospect of a new life started to capture their imagination a few months ago when they replied to a small advertisement in a local newspaper.

Their applications were answered by a retired Naval officer at Horndean. He had friends in the Falkland Islands, he explained, who wanted British lads—preferably sons of the soil—to go out there to work for at least five years.

ADVENTURE

They will get free passage each way and will be paid a wage about equal to that paid in Britain. They will be able to supplement it with extra cash from peat cutting and fencing.

ON THEIR OWN

From the two Scots the seven South Countrymen have been hearing of the life that is in store for them. They will be shepherds of the flocks of up to 2,000 sheep; and for a part of the year will be out, miles from anywhere, on their own except for the sheep.

Their home will be a shanty, they will cook their own food, and when they want fresh meat, they will slaughter one of the flock.

For most of the year all the shepherds live together in a central bunkhouse.

Said George Douglas (25), of Cowdenknowes, Mains, Earlston, Berwickshire, who is going back for another five years: "Life is what you make it. In the farm centre, where some of the older shepherds have their wives, we manage to get along very well. There is an Army film projector and we have dances.

TWO-DAY VOYAGE TO TOWN

"All stores are brought to the sheep station and there is no need to go to Port Stanley, the nearest town. Anyway, it is a two-day voyage by boat and when I was there I never went into town once."

Returning with Douglas is William Macbeth (22), of Lynchat, Kingussie, Inverness-shire. They met during the annual West Island sports meetings which are held, by rotation, on the big farms.

On Fox Bay West farm, where Douglas is going, there are 31,000 sheep.

The Hanne S is carrying 500 tons of timber cargo from Sweden to Port Stanley, and a general cargo from Southampton of iron, pipes, tinned food, motor vehicles and diesel oil. Master of the ship, which has a crew of 15, is Captain Mogens Tonder (36), a handsome 6ft. tall Dane.

ROUND VOYAGE

The round voyage will last three months, ending at London with the unloading of wool and hides from the Falkland Islands.

" To be a farmer's boy " . . . that is the idea behind the long sea voyage of these nine young lads who are going to the Falkland Islands to take up jobs on a sheep farm. The nine young men, photographed on board the Hanne S today, are (left to right): Roger Edwards, Albert J. Hatch, Ivan A. Aylward, Claude H. Triggs, Mervyn C. Muller, Tony E. R. Talbot, Frank W. Martin, William MacBeth and George M. Douglas.—" Echo " photo.

CHAPTER 2

PACKE BROTHERS AND COMPANY

Having arrived in Stanley, it soon became apparent that it would be some days before I would be able to travel to Fox Bay, a large sheep station with which I had accepted a five year contract and the reason for coming 8,000 miles. With time to spare I took the opportunity of helping to unload the cargo from the hold of the *Hanne S*, which included clothing, provisions, and a large quantity of cigarettes, wines and spirits.

Some found it thirsty work, and applied one of the tricks of the trade to get a free tot of whisky. The bottles, packed tightly in wooden cases were each encased in a straw sleeve. When dropped sharply on one corner the nearest bottle fractured and allowed the whisky to trickle out, filtered through the straw and caught in cupped hands, disregarding the possibility that it could contain sharp slivers of broken glass. Had the miscreants been spotted by Bill Grierson, the one and only Customs Officer, whose ever-watchful eye missed few indiscretions, he would have suffered the emotional pain of a Court appearance, the result of which would have been broadcast to the town.

Sunday was particularly quiet with all the shops closed and the bars were permitted to open for only one hour, at lunchtime. With the Police Station just one street away, it was a sufficient reminder to ensure that an hour was exactly sixty minutes long.

The only exception to the Glory Hour rule was at the Mon Star, a small pub, about two miles out of town to the east, seemingly built to provide refreshment for picnickers and fishermen.

It was early evening on my first Sunday when I met Willy MacBeth. His return to Port San Carlos had been delayed and together we agreed to walk to the Mon Star. The road was poorly maintained, characterised by loose gravel and potholes. Motorised traffic consisted mainly of Land Rovers and a few motor cycles. We ambled along, talking and caring little about the passage of time and the pub was in darkness when we finally arrived. Wally assured me that it was only to be expected, the weather was cold and damp, with Winter about to set in, and the landlord would not have expected to see customers, sometimes for days on end. A sharp rap on the door brought the expected response and we were ushered in with a cheery greeting from the Landlord. By the light of an oil lamp he poured out our drinks and then ambled off to another room to prepare a Tilley lamp that would provide a light bright enough to enable us to play a game of darts.

At about nine o'clock, just as we were getting weary of walking up and down to the dart board, with a lack of interest that ensured we maintained a pitifully low score, the door opened and in walked two additional customers, to the delight of the Landlord, Willy and I. They, like us, had walked from Stanley and we not only had two opponents to play at darts, but two female opponents, perhaps it was not going to be such a dull evening after all.

Willy and I made our own arrangements for our walk back to town, much later than anticipated, but not before agreeing to meet at the Rose Hotel the next evening. It was not until then, much to his amusement, that I discovered that our companions during the latter part of the previous evening had been two of the most notorious ladies of the entire islands, in whose company we should never wish to be seen if we wanted to retain our self respect. I was still on a very steep learning curve. It turned out to be one of those rare occasions when I was thankful for a dark winter's evening.

One of Carrie McLeod's residents was a Welshman who, although based in Stanley, was a member of the Falkland Islands Dependencies Survey Team. He loved nothing better than to pass an evening putting the world to rights, particularly after spending a few hours in the Falkland Club which was one of the two "Members only" clubs in the islands.

One evening, while I was there, he returned home very much at peace with himself. We sat around the ample kitchen table engaged in a discussion on which we had little, or no knowledge at all. We were interrupted regularly by the cuckoo-clock which hung on the wall above the large, peat burning cooking range. The cuckoo sounded out its rough estimate of the time. Ten o'clock was followed by 10.30, then eleven o'clock. Each time, Taffy's concentration on the subject in hand was interrupted, as in order to be heard, we had to wait until the offending bird had made sufficient exits. Taffy, determined to have the last word, was as defiant as the cuckoo. When the sound of his last call had died away, Taffy put the little catch on the door, mumbling that he was not going to be beaten by a wooden bird, then sat down to carry on the discussion, believing that in securing the door, he also stopped the mating call of the cuckoo.

How wrong he was. This one, as he was to find to his cost, worked independently of the door. At precisely 11.30 there was a whirring noise followed by a muffled clunk as Carrie's cuckoo was dispatched in a number of pieces to the floor of the clock, which took more than a passing observation to explain the reason for the broken timepiece to Carrie the next morning. The expressed willingness to purchase a replacement did little to placate the most genial of landladies.

Of the original nine passengers on the *Hanne S*, only Ivan Aylward and I were to work for the same company. After much discussion and two attempts to have us flown out to Fox Bay, both of which had to be abandoned because of the weather conditions, it was finally arranged that we would travel the one hundred or so miles on board the *Philomel*, a small inshore cargo vessel of about one hundred tons. She was not equipped to carry passengers so it was necessary for us to leave Stanley early in the morning.

We travelled south west for some hours, passing some of the outlying but inhabited islands, all the signs around us suggesting that the weather was going to deteriorate. All too often it seemed that the wind got up with the sun as dawn broke and went down with the sun at dusk. For the *Philomel*, travelling after dark was unwise in the extreme. Our skipper decided that it was incautious to make the journey across the Falkland Sound, separating the West Falklands from the East and instead, anchored in Bull Roads, a sheltered, deep water group of small islands that offered a safe haven from the sudden storms. Many seafarers had reason to be thankful for the shelter that they gave.

Story had it that on one occasion the *Fitzroy*, on her way to the West Falklands ran into foul weather which caused her Captain, Freddie White, a degree of concern. Aware that one of his passengers was renowned for his seamanship and knowledge of the islands, he sent for him and asked his advice. In thick fog and driving rain, the *Fitzroy* was taken into Bull Roads and anchored for the night. The next morning when it became light, to his horror, Freddie White , found the bow of his ship towering over the dry land of an island. To make matters worse, he could see no way out. He hastily sent for the ageing skipper saying, "You got us in here, now get us out". Which of course, he did.

We made our way into Fox Bay Harbour at about eleven o'clock the next morning, having spent a somewhat sleepless night in the cramped eating quarters of the *Philomel* which was all too reminiscent of the days aboard the *Hanne S* shortly after leaving England, the real difference on this occasion being the relative calm of the islands. It was a welcome sight. The changeable weather was now providing a calm and tranquil scene which I was going to see many times through the next few years and would leave me with many memories which are impossible to erase.

Fox Bay East, with Packe's Port Howard and Dunnose Head represented the total holdings, in the Falklands, of absentee landlord Packe Brothers and Company Limited. The three farms totalled about 150,000 acres and supported 50,000 sheep.

The settlement was the most important on the West Falklands. As its name implies it lay on the east side of a half mile wide harbour, the entrance of which was dominated by two towering hills that rose steeply from the beach and were known as the East and West Heads.

At the settlement itself, the Manager's house was situated at one end of the green on the side of a gentle slope above the shearing shed and jetty. At the other end of the green and close to the beach stood the accommodation for the single men, known as the cookhouse, with fifteen single rooms, a kitchen, mess and washroom facilities. Between these two homes stood three houses for the married men, one of whom was the Foreman, Mike Murphy.

Like most farms, it employed three categories of workers. Navvies worked in and around the settlement, maintaining fences and outbuildings, when not required to help with the sheep work. Outside Shepherds, as the title implies, lived perhaps five or even ten miles away from the settlement, daily tending the flocks of sheep for which they were responsible, in the vast farmland. Finally the Roustabout, who had his own troop of horses, worked the sheep that were close to the settlement, but also worked with the navvies when there was no sheep work to be done.

At the top of the green stood the Government-owned wireless station and post office and the homes of the West Falklands doctor and his guide. Chris Perry. With the wireless operator cum Postmaster, Eric Smith, the three represented the total Government staff on the West Falklands, and consequently gave Fox Bay East its importance over the other six main sheep stations.

Packe's Port Howard to the north, some seven hours horse ride away, was looked after by just two men, father and son. Gordon and George Stewart, with additional support when needed from shepherds and roustabouts from other parts of the farm.

Dunnose Head to the extreme west, was another eight hours horse ride away and, like Port Howard, shared the one Manager, Wickham Clements.

With Bill Paice as Foreman, Dunnose Head had a complement of three single men and a cook. An outside shepherd lived at Shallow Harbour, an hour's ride further west from the settlement, with his wife and two children.

Bill Paice was married, with one son and two daughters. His house was ten minutes walk "Up the track", from the settlement, which, in addition to the cookhouse, had a shearing shed, sheep dip, provision store, tractor shed and boat house. Like all settlements, it was situated close to the beach, in a well protected harbour.

It was only on arrival at Fox Bay that Ivan and I learnt that we were both to work in Dunnose Head, following a brief stay of three weeks in Fox Bay. We were given rooms in the cookhouse and joined the resident gang for lunch - it was to be the first of many. A predictable menu for every cookhouse in the islands, roast chops for breakfast with onion rings and gravy, roast shoulder or leg of mutton for lunch, with potatoes if we were lucky, together with tinned peas or beans and more gravy. The evening meal was equally predictable, more of the same but this time cold, with plain bread.

After lunch I went out to explore my new surroundings. I was anxious to get to work, having endured a lengthy period of enforced idleness. Regardless of the direction in which I gazed, all I could see was open land-scape with a backdrop of rolling hills. Had I done the right thing? Not for the first time the misgivings were creeping in but there was no turning back.

CHAPTER 3

OUT AND ABOUT

Although it was Saturday and work had finished for the weekend at mid-day, Mike Murphy came walking across the green with the intention of taking a tractor and trailer out to the camp, to bring home some peat, from a bog about two miles from the settlement. Each household required about two hundred cubic yards of peat a year, for heating and cooking and the cookhouse needed twice as much. I eagerly joined Mike, pleased to be doing something both new and worthwhile.

It was impossible to be isolated. Falkland Island people, whatever their job and wherever they were, relied on other people for news and information. To pass a shepherd's house without calling in was unheard of, an insult. Without doubt an extra place would have been laid at the table, regardless of the time of day. Visiting was a part of daily life and within the confines of the settlement at Fox Bay, acted as a transition between the life we had known at home, and the almost solitary existence that we were about to experience.

Solitude enabled us to see and hear all that was going on around us, which hitherto, had been excluded by what we had grown up to expect as being part of every day life. It also provided the opportunity to seek out the characteristics of the islands, many of them unique, that were encountered every day and soon to be taken for granted, I wanted to find out what I could of the islands and the people who had, for better or for worse, accepted me as one of them.

The journey to the peat bog gave me another opportunity to look at the landscape. Rolling hills and high rocky ridges with natural boundaries provided by the rugged coastline, typical of many totally enclosed land masses; towering sea-lashed cliffs, shallow and often calm sand and shingle bays, lowland peninsulas and jagged rocks jutting out into the sea, often submerged at high tide, presenting a danger to an unwary sailor. In the harbour were three small islands providing winter feed for the few milking cows, winter grazing for horses and home for a few rock-hopper penguins. Inland, fences divided one piece of camp from the next and one station from another, sometimes resulting in individual pieces of camp extending into thousands of acres. The small paddocks around the settlement often enclosed fifty or sixty acres, larger than a generous smallholding at home.

The soil varied from a sandy loam to a deep red peat, often extending more than ten feet in depth. Much of the terrain was solid rock particularly in areas a few hundred feet above sea level. The highest point was Mount Usborne on the East Falklands which rose to 2,300 feet. An unusual feature, often found in a valley that started high up in the hills and went down towards the sea, were stone-runs, a river-like formation, stretching up to one hundred yards wide and half a mile long resulting from some geological reformation countless centuries ago and difficult, if not impossible, to cross. Made up of boulders that varied in size from mere stones weighing two or three pounds to huge boulders up to four or five tons in weight.

The vegetation was poor with the wet peaty areas covered in a long white grass which was of no nutritional value for the sheep. Diddle-dee, fachine bushes and fern made up much of the ground cover on the higher ground. The sheep were obliged to feed on the short cropped grass of the valleys and hillside and forage for whatever weed shoots they could, in order to survive, which gave rise to the relatively small number of sheep in comparison with the total acreage available.

In the camp, communication with Stanley was mainly by radio transmitter. particularly those on the West Falkland and remote islands. Communication between the farms and the outside shepherds was by land line, forever breaking down. Days or even weeks would sometimes pass before someone got around to "riding the line", looking for the break.

The prevailing climatic conditions dominated the lives of the population. Strong winds, rarely less than twenty knots on good days and thirty five, gusting to eighty, blew on bad ones. Summer temperatures rarely rose above seventy degrees Fahrenheit. Driving rain was inescapable and the main feature of the Falkland winter. Falls of snow were light in comparison with its latitudinal counterpart of the Western Isles of Scotland.

The Falkland Islands is the only group of note in the South Atlantic. Although the East and West Islands account for most of the 4,600 square miles of land, there are in all some three hundred islands, of which only ten or fifteen are inhabited. Many of them populated only by sheep and the ever-present abundance of wild birds.

At all stages of its life cycle, the upland goose played a big part in ensuring that our diet had some variety. The goose egg, gosling and mature bird all found themselves on the meal table during the spring and summer months. The upland goose carried a bounty on its beak, four or five could eat as much grass as a sheep. The bounty was a ready source of pocket-money for boys living in the camp. The geese were at their most vulnerable when shedding their feathers.

The preferred method of bringing a fleeing bird to the ground was with the bolas regularly used on the mainland in Uruguay, Argentina and Patagonia by both the police and the gaucho alike, to impede the departure of a fleeing suspect, horse or sheep. The bolas used by the boys in the Falklands were made with three chunky knee-joints of a bullock after it had been picked clean by birds and bleached white by the wind and rain, joined with cords of equal length. The assailant, holding firmly onto one of the weights, spun the bolas horizontally at head height, before releasing it in the direction of the intended captive.

The boys, quite naturally, became very experienced at bringing a goose back to earth with a bump entangled in the bolas, the most tender finding themselves the subject of a roast lunch. A boat travelling round the camp invariable returned to Stanley with a few dozen geese for family and friends living in the town. The radio transmitter was used to relay the message to the intended recipient that they should go down to the harbour to meet the boat on her arrival.

The kelp goose, almost as common as the upland, was inclined to stay close to the beach and to the settlement. Unlike the upland goose, it was a protected species, inedible, and very tame. Its protection in law did little to save it from the casual visitor who, armed with a hunting rifle, came ashore for a few hours hunting, unable to distinguish one breed of goose from another could often be seen heading back towards his boat weighed down with half a dozen protected geese.

The gull was, of course, the most common of the scavengers, but the straited caracara or Johnny Rook was the most popular, seeming to prefer the company of people to that of other birds. Although keeping its distance, it took delight in flying a few yards ahead of the traveller, or sitting on a convenient fence post to watch work going on in and around the settlement. It was not uncommon for them to assume the characteristics of the British magpie and steal shiny objects small enough to be carried in its vice-like claws. Equally he was not adverse to stealing a beret blown off in the wind - very few people wore a hat likely to be caught by the wind - by waiting for the owner to get within a few feet and then, firmly holding on to the stolen head-piece, carry it forward a further ten or twenty yards and so it went on until either the offended owner or the bird gave up what was for one a game and the other a most aggravating experience.

The bald headed eagle or turkey buzzard was far less friendly and flew off at the first sight of people. It was both destructive and vicious, forever on the lookout for a sickly lamb or a sheep that had got over on its back and was unable to return to its feet. Goslings and penguin chicks left unattended for a minute were all at its mercy. During the lambing season the shepherd kept a watchful eye open for a circling buzzard, knowing that it was waiting for the right moment to strike.

Because of their destructive nature, these birds of prey also carried a bounty on their heads but it was only a lucky encounter that enabled the boys to entangle one with a bolas. It was for a chance shot at a turkey that the shotgun was placed within easy reach of the back door of many homes in the camp but even that presented the unwary with an additional hazard. When sensing danger the turkey invariably vomited the entire contents of its stomach, irrespective of who might be underneath to benefit from the experience. The reason was not by way of retaliation but because its reduced weight enabled it to rise quickly out of danger.

Of the four or five species of penguin found in the islands, the gentoo and the tiny rock-hopper were the most common. The latter would scrape out a hole in the sandy soil of an isolated island in which to scurry when disturbed, but at nesting time they were equally as happy sharing their rocky nesting ground with the Dominican gulls and other sea birds. Despite its diminutive size, the rock-hopper was still the most vicious of the species.

It was not unusual to find penguin rookeries accommodating three or four thousand birds, who returned each year to the same nesting ground which could be clearly identified by the total absence of vegetation and the reddish grey accumulation of lime, not to mention the smell which, with a gentle breeze in the right direction could be identified a mile away. The courtship began in early spring as the penguins flood ashore with much squawking and bowing. The noise was quite deafening and carried on from dawn until dusk. As each couple paired up, the ritual of courtship began in earnest and the nest making started. Sticks and twigs from diddle-dee bushes and rubbish gathered up from the beach were brought the few yards inland and formed into a bowl-shaped nest.

Frustrating yet fascinating to watch was the care and attention paid to the positioning of each piece of nesting material, with repeated attempts to get it right. Having satisfied itself that it had found the best position, the penguin marched off to find another piece, only to have the original stolen by another pair engaged in the same occupation nearby, so the process went on until all were satisfied and the business of laying eggs and incubation could begin. Both parent birds took turns to incubate the eggs while the other went off in search of food for itself, sometimes for days at a time. Having hatched, the parents continue the dual role of feeding the small balls of fluff by regurgitation. When not feeding, the young could be seen perched precariously on the parents' feet. It was a dangerous time for the young. Left unattended, they became prey for the ever-hungry buzzards.

Each pair produced two eggs, about twice the size of a large chicken egg, completely round and encased in a very hard off-white shell, so hard it was possible to throw an egg high into the air and let it fall without breaking. If robbed of their eggs early in the season the penguins would nest again so it was with that knowledge that two or three hundred eggs were packed into huge saddle bags, surrounded by diddle-dee and fern leaves and transported back to the settlement, largely undamaged by the rough jostling on the back of a horse. The yoke, almost brick red in colour, had a strong fish like flavour and varied considerably in keeping with the diet of the penguin. Colonies of seal and sea-lion inhabited the tussock islands where they remained largely undisturbed. The bull elephant seal was the largest, whose trunk-like snout extended and retracted as it snorted and grunted its disapproval when disturbed.

Smelt and mullet were the two most common on-shore fish caught and eaten. Trout was introduced into freshwater streams in the early 1950s and provided an exciting sport and pastime.

Livestock, food, wool and people all depended in a direct way on the sea. Eight to ten knot tides were commonplace in harbours and bays. Local knowledge was essential for the small vessels that moved around the settlements, many of them owned and operated by those who lived on the small outlying islands, who, without their boats, would be unable to operate effectively or economically.

The islands were quite well charted but they could not take account of the shifting sand and shingle banks close inshore, which frequently caused the smaller boats to become grounded and then obliged to remain there until the next high tide lifted them clear. For every grounding or accident at sea there were ten near misses, high winds and fast running tides a witness to every one. Many were caused by the heart ruling the head and the situation only saved by God's grace.

PEAT CUTTING

CHAPTER 4

THE TASTE OF SALT WATER

Ron Tunnel had been at Fox Bay East for two seasons before we arrived and was courting Paula Bridge, who was maid at the home of Fox Bay West Manager Charlie Robertson, a big, deep-voiced, no-nonsense man of few words but firm action.

One evening after work, Ron, Rita Davies, who held a similar position to that of Paula with Mr. Clements, and I decided to go and visit Paula. The girls had been at school together in Stanley. It had all the hallmarks of being a rough night when Ron went over to see Mike Murphy and ask permission to use the dinghy. Mike offered cautionary notes about the weather but, reluctantly, agreed.

The row across the harbour usually took about ten minutes. The tide had started to rise and would take us into the harbour rather than out towards the East Head and the open sea. Ron expressed the view that the cross wind from the north west would cause us most difficulty, but nothing that was insurmountable. For my part and that of Rita, both new to the experience of venturing out in a boat after dark, we relied on his judgement.

The tide being in our favour, we set out, intending first to row out towards the East Head, keeping close into the shore and out of the tidal flow and then make a run with the tide, across to the other side of the harbour, hopefully ending up somewhere close to the Fox Bay West jetty. It worked well at first, the tide taking us back into the middle of the harbour and across to the other side. However, once clear of the lee of the land the wind started to take the bow of the dinghy and bring us side-on to the tide, presenting the danger that we could either capsize or, if turned right around, be taken out to sea, the very place our worst fears would be realised. We battled hard with just one pair of oars and both Ron and I rowing. The swell in the centre of the harbour presented added difficulties as it lifted, first the bow and then the stern, clear of the water.

Tension began to enter Ron's voice. It was pitch black and the driving rain from a sudden squall made matters worse. Our only hope was to pull hard, keep the bow into the wind and hope that we were making progress. We looked for landmarks that would tell us where we were. There were three islands within the harbour that we had to look for, all of them more than halfway across. One, the Fox Bay East Tussock island, would mean that we were too far into the harbour, but on the other hand safely through the pull of the rising tide. Sight of the other two islands, which were close together, would mean that although clear of the tide, we were on the seaward side of the jetty, facing a near gale force wind. To be close to Horse Island, the middle of the three, would take us dangerously close to a shallow reef that ran out towards the mainland. Suddenly and simultaneously we saw the skyline of Horse Island and felt a bump as the bow of the dinghy touched the reef. Ron shouted "Pull, and put your weight towards the stern", the intention being to lift the boat clear of the reef, we all held our breath and pulled as Ron, still trying to row with one oar, threw his weight towards the stern. There was no time to look, just pull and hope.

The wind eased as we moved between the island and the beach. We had been thrown clear of the reef and out of danger. We made the jetty and secured the boat, too exhausted to speak, too relieved to be frightened. There had been no time before, but now the emotion of fear was suppressed by the emotion of relief.

Paula thought we had turned back. Ron had telephoned her before we set out but we had been so long in getting there she had assumed we had turned back.

We went to Paula's sitting room. She was allowed to have visitors but they had to leave by ten o'clock. That presented no difficulty, Ron and I had to turn to at six o'clock and we would not have been able to do that without a good night's sleep, even with every muscle aching it would have made no difference, already we were exhausted.

The problems did not just stop at the possibility of being late for work, we would also have to explain the absence of the dinghy. We had no intention of repeating the danger we had just experienced. The reality of the situation we had been in was only just beginning to sink in. The wind would have to drop and the sky clear, to allow the moon to show through the clouds, to provide us with some light on the return journey and that all had to happen before the tide turned. I hoped the memory of the unhappy experience would serve to temper my enthusiasm for subsequent boat trips during bad weather. Another mistake!

The weather made no attempt to meet our requirements and at ten o'clock, the diesel generator which provided the electricity would shut down, leaving us all in darkness. We agreed on contingency plans. They were that Rita would try to get a few hours sleep on the settee in Paula's room and hope that no one would find out, while Ron and I would go to the cookhouse where we would, hopefully, also get some sleep.

The latest time that we could leave was 4 a.m. because, although that would leave us plenty of time to get across the harbour, if we were unable to use the boat, we would have sufficient time to walk around the head of the harbour and that would take us all of two hours.

We left the girls and went to the cookhouse, where we explained our plight and were invited to stay as we had asked. We turned down the invitation to have a bed, fearing we may not wake in time, instead we accepted blankets and an offer of an alarm clock and settled down to what proved to be a fitful sleep.

After tossing and turning on the hard floor, it seemed as if we had only just dropped off to sleep when the alarm sounded, three a.m. The cook had just got up to start his day, there was just time for us to rake out the ash from the still glowing peat fire, drink a cup of lukewarm coffee and leave.

The wind was still blowing as badly as it had been the previous evening, as we made our way down across the green. The Manager's house was in darkness. I led the way to the back door and opened it carefully; there was never any need to lock doors at night, particularly in the camp. I reached inside, feeling for the light switch. Finding it, I pushed it down, a faint light flickered into life. Ron whispered sharply, "Put that bloody light out quick!". Unknown to me, the light worked directly off the generator, switching the light on automatically started the generator, and not too quietly at that. Hence Ron's reason for reacting so crisply.

Our way into Paula's room now had to be made with the aid of matches which, fortunately, we both had. Tapping gently on the door we hoped to wake Rita who, as far as we were concerned, was asleep on the settee. No reply, opening the door quietly and with the aid of another match we looked in. It was not difficult to see that the room was empty. Now what do we do? Ron, who by this time had come into the room behind me, spotted a note on the mantelpiece. A short note, saying that Rita had gone to sleep with Paula; but where?

Ron, quite genuinely, did not seem to know the way but stressed that it was upstairs and the second room on the left off the elongated landing. Under protest and having tried to convince him that it would have been far better if he went to find them, I made my way up the dark stairway feeling my way along the banister, around the bend in the stairs and onto the landing which, on striking another match, I was able to see opened onto a wide hall running the full length of the house with a number of doors leading off each side. Counting the doors and whispering to Ron for confirmation that he had said the second door on the left, he in the meantime having come part of the way up the stairs behind me, I went to the appropriate door, knocked gently, I only had to hold my hand close to the door, the knock came from the nervous tremor in my wrist.

A muffled response came from inside the room as I tried to quietly convey the message that it was time to go and that we were going to have to walk all the way around, to what was known colloquially as "The other side". Unable to clearly hear what was being said, I opened the door.

I had checked with Ron the room that the girls were expected to be in but despite those careful and deliberate checks, when the light came on in the room it was not Paula or Rita who was sitting up in bed, making enquiries regarding my presence. I like to think that, given time, I can make an artic- ulate response to most questions, but on that occasion I was left with little choice but to talk fast and I did, seemingly successfully because, Mr Charlie, as he was known, got up and went to the second door on the right of the stairs to wake the girls.

Needless to say, we travelled as fast as we could in the early dawn light, for two reasons, one to put space between me and Mr Charlie, the second to be back in the settlement in time to change into our working clothes and present ourselves for work.

There were some difficult questions that would need answering in the fullness of time, fortunately, we were spared a detailed inquisition as to why the dinghy was still on the other side of the harbour. For my part, at that particular time, it was going to stay there until it was both calm and daylight.

CHAPTER 5

OVERLAND TO DUNNOSE HEAD

Our stay in Fox Bay passed quickly. Mr Clements was in Packe's Port Howard and under Mike's direction we involved ourselves in dipping the last of the season's sheep which had been in the paddocks, adjacent to the settlement, during the summer. It was a hard and tiring job that fortunately took place only once a year.

We spent some days helping with the annual cull of sheep whose wool had become coarse through age or inbreeding. It was not unusual for some farms to cull out as many as 1,000 sheep each year, it was awesome to see the carcasses of that number of sheep being scavenged by many times their number of gulls and caracara. Only the skins were saved, like the wool, for pressing into bales and shipment to the United Kingdom.

Essential repairs to the fences and pens around the settlement were usually carried out before the worst of the winter weather set in. Left to last were those jobs that could be done in the comparative warmth of the sheds, like the lengthy job of cleaning the slatted floor of the shearing shed of the accumulation of manure from the sheep which had been packed tightly in the shed the night before shearing to improve the warmth, thereby making them easier to shear.

The day was warm and bright when we left for Chartres on our way to Dunnose Head. Although Chartres was an entirely separate sheep station, it was always the accepted, and expected, practice that travellers would be offered the help and hospitality of each farm that happened to be on the route of the traveller. Ivan, having been brought up in the heavily-populated areas of Portsmouth, was not looking forward to the prospects of working where there were even fewer people than there had been in Fox Bay and already was beginning to regret that he ever left home.

Our transport that day was a former World War Two bren gun carrier, which had the advantage of speed over the conventional tracked vehicle and was equally adept at coping with the changing terrain. The track to Chartres was poor. The wheel tracks had cut deep into the sandy soil on which grew the common white grass that helped to prevent soil erosion in the strong winds, but the small tufts of grass also ensured that the journey was far from smooth. During dry weather, good progress could be made but tracks were soon transformed into swamp during the Winter. There was one small stream to cross at Bull Flat, but the Chartres River, a moderately shallow tributary about six miles south of the settlement, was difficult to cross as the river bed was made up of large stones. A bridge further downstream was unsuitable for vehicles with heavy loads. It was a case of "steady as she goes" and giving the largest of the rocks a wide berth.

It was lunchtime when we arrived at the "top cookhouse", an outside shepherds house, which formed part of the Chartres sheep station. In former days it had housed a number of single men, but was now home to a shepherd, his wife and two children.

Most of the Chartres gang was there, they had just finished dipping the last of their sheep. We had lunch with them and unloaded our luggage from the bren gun carrier, which then set off on its return journey to Fox Bay. For me it was an opportunity to meet old friends, for no fewer than four of the Chartres team came from neighbouring villages to my own in Hampshire, we had all attended the same schools.

We travelled the rest of the way to Chartres by tractor and trailer. Although pot-holed and rough, the road was firm, and we took little time in getting to the settlement, where we were to spend the night.

We had crossed the Chartres river at its shallowest point. The settlement itself was situated where the river opened up to provide a harbour, with sufficient depth of water to enable the cargo boats to come in and pick up the bales of wool and skins. Not all farms had deep water jetties, even fewer had sufficient water at both high and low tide. It was frequently necessary for very wide flat-bottomed boats, known as skows, to take the wool from the jetty and then be towed, by motor-boat, out into deep water where the parent boat lay at anchor, waiting to lift the bales from the skows into its own hold.

Christmas Harbour separated the farm from the Dunnose Head camp and it was from that point that travellers to Dunnose Head would be taken across by motor-boat. Although only about 150 yards wide, it was subject to eight to ten knot tides, when the tide was at full flow. From time to time it was necessary to swim horses across at this point, calling for considerable skill by the boatman. A fast running tide could quickly tire a horse and carry it much further than it could be safely expected to swim.

It was just after eleven o'clock the next morning when word came to the cookhouse that two riders, with additional horses, had been seen approaching the Point. This was our cue to be put across the river, with two large suitcases each and, as we were shortly to find out, a sufficient load to require two horses for the four hour ride to Dunnose Head.

Jimmy Duncan, the Chartres Foreman, had prepared the motor-boat in readiness to take us to meet Bill Paice and his son George, who, although only twelve years old, was expected to take part in much of the farm work. For most boys starting work on the sheep farm, their first job was that of "wool boy", carrying the fleece from the shearer to the grading table, but their ability to do many of the jobs around the farm was learnt long before they finished their schooling.

It was damp and cold in comparison with the previous day, and the wind much stronger. We were glad of the limited shelter provided by the very steep-sided but short valley at the place where we had been put ashore by the boat. With Ivan Aylward and I being totally inexperienced, it took nearly an hour to prepare ourselves for our first mammoth horse ride.

The uneven track and the bumping, swaying load on the horses that we were leading resulted in half hourly stops to check the loads had not cut into the horses or chafed the skin, causing sores that would take days to heal.

We passed the Gun Hill shanty, where Bill and George had spent the previous night. Close by and nearly on the beach was a pile of crudely placed stones, claimed to be the grave of an old seafarer by the name of Jim Brockway, who had died on board a sailing ship almost one hundred years before and brought ashore for burial. Locals dismissed the story as untrue. Men with time on their hands had tried to dig up Brock's remains and finding nothing there, after digging down a few feet, gave up the search, but most folk preferred to believe it was the resting place of the sailor and kept the spot tidy, mainly in fear that the spirit of "Old Brock" might come visiting the shanty on stormy nights.

We travelled on, three men, a boy and six horses, one behind the other, keeping to the coast line all the way, until we came to the, "Narrows", how aptly named they were! A steep-sided valley, with just horse and sheep tracks, called the Devils Steps, leading down into the valley bottom, which was almost at sea level, about a quarter of a mile wide, stretching the other way from King George Bay to the innermost reaches of the Isthmus Cove and Port Philomel. About three quarters of a mile long, with two very large lakes in the middle, both ends of the valley were clearly visible. At the northern end was a barren and deserted gentoo penguin nesting site.

The way out of the Narrows and up to the Cattle Ground camp was not as steep as that which had led us in, although we were still obliged to lead our horses, it was far less frightening. We were still one and a half hours ride from the settlement but the remainder of the journey was pleasantly uneventful and we arrived at Bill's house in time for tea. The house was overshadowed by a large macrocarpa tree. It was the only tree I was to see in the Falklands, although there was a small plantation of conifers at the Hill Cove sheep station, away to the north west.

In the early evening we went down the track to the cookhouse which was to be home for me for the next two years. The only other residents were Tommy, or Two-bob Skilling, and Alfie Banks.

Tom Skilling was our cook. Alfie had arrived from Fox Bay just a few days previous and although he was quite a few years older than Ivan or I, he was still very much a new boy in this part of the island.

The winter months with their limited number of daylight hours were to be spent in bringing home the peat, cleaning out the shed and maintaining the farm buildings.

Among my many jobs was that of tractor driver, which brought with it a new dimension in maintenance and repair of the ageing American built "Cletrac", which at that time was our only mechanical transport. The trailer had wheels on the front and half tracks on the rear, an invaluable aid in crossing small streams with steep-sided banks.

Our first visitor, a few weeks after we arrived, was Mr Clements, making what he called his annual pilgrimage to that part of the farm. Although very short in stature, he had rugged features, with a very positive square jaw giving him the image of a no- nonsense disciplinarian, masking the fairness with which he treated all the station hands. Alfie was more than a trifle apprehensive about meeting the Boss, although both knew each other well. Too well for Alfie's liking, which gave rise to much of his apprehension, for there was in Alfie more than a hint of a guilty conscience. It transpired that he had been cutting peat a few months earlier at the Hawks Nest shanty and Mr Clements arranged to take him a large quantity of tinned food when he next passed that way. Unfortunately for Alfie the visit coincided with him sleeping off the effects of what had been a very thirsty weekend. The Boss, not wishing to disturb him, carefully stacked the stores all around his reclining form on the bunk bed, and quietly left, leaving Alfie to wake up in his own good time and realise that he had been caught out. Hence his embarrassment, which was never to be completely dispelled. Mr Clements preferred to drop the hint from time to time that he had not forgotten.

It was during the visit that Ivan Aylward, unable to come to terms with the quiet and absence of people, asked if he could return to Fox Bay with Mr Clements, which he did and after a few months there, terminated his contract and returned home. It was not unusual for young men to break their contract and find employment on another farm, but few found it sufficiently intolerable to force them to leave the islands within two years of their arrival.

A few weeks later Two-bob, after much heart searching, made a decision, it was time to take one of his infrequent and extended winter holidays in town. Like many of his contempories who had been brought up in Stanley but spent most of their working life on the farms, he retained a desire to return at infrequent intervals, not just to visit friends and relations but to feel, once again, the marked difference between life in town and the comparative loneliness of the camp. He was replaced as temporary cook by Ben Evans, also from Fox Bay. Ben was a very small and fiery tempered man. In addition to lacking many of Tom's culinary skills he was always keen to avoid waste that, in turn, would keep down the cost of the stores used in the cookhouse. The cost was later apportioned to each man living in the cookhouse and deducted from his wage at the end of the month.

Perhaps it was unfair to say Ben was always thrifty, it was never without purpose. For him, the period of austerity, in which we were all obliged to share, was dedicated to saving money that would pay for his next holiday in town, which, like Tom's, took place every two or three years and was mainly devoted to one continuous pub crawl, only to be drawn to a conclusion when his money ran out, it was then, with rather a heavy heart, he made his way back out to camp, to embark on another period of frugal existence. It was under Ben's guidance and repeated reminder, that I stopped taking sugar in tea and coffee. As he said, it's "Bloomin' expensive ya'know".

One Saturday lunchtime during Tom's absence, I was eating a piece of jam tart that Ben had "constructed". He and Alfie sat talking of old islanders that they both knew. The pastry, for want of a better name, was like a piece of board, I ate that which had jam on it and left a small piece, which was about two inches square. During the course of their conversation Joe made repeated furtive glances at the crust on my plate, until he could contain himself no longer. With a stabbing finger aimed at the offending crust, he barked: "Ain't ya going to eat that? Bloomin' waste ya' know".

Ben rarely swore, but much of what he said was prefixed by, "Bloomin'" which, coupled with his habit of dropping the "H" from anything he said, resulted in us riding "Bloomin' 'orses" and people being "Bloomin' 'orrible". Tom's return from town some weeks later was most welcome, only equalled by Ben's departure back to Fox Bay the next day.

CHAPTER 6

A NIGHT WITH OLD BROCK

The first test of my engineering skills came when the Cletrac developed a fault in the gearbox, not surprisingly, right at the time when it was needed to take fencing material to the shepherd at Shallow Harbour. It was a feat of endurance to get it into gear and once in almost impossible to get out. So with the aid of a greatly abridged maintenance manual, much of it obliterated by greasy thumb prints of a bygone service, I set to and dismantled the clutch and gear box, with only Alfie to assist me in lifting the heavy pieces, assistance that was given grudgingly. He much preferred to make gates and doors, or anything else for that matter, including a rocking horse for Bill Paice's youngest daughter, Joan, in the comparative warmth of the carpenter's shop over which he was king.

Carefully laying out the pieces of the gearbox in the order in which they came off, I dismantled it completely, replaced bearings that showed sign of wear from the crates of spare parts, both new and used, that had come with the tractor from Fox Bay, at a time when it was already admitted that the best of her days were passed.

Dismantling it was the easy part, it took some time, largely working on my own, before I reached the stage of having put it all back together and it was ready to be tried out. The gear lever and the clutch moved freely, which gave me sufficient confidence to start it up, a job fraught with difficulties as, being an old vehicle, it was not fitted with an electric starter, but the all too familiar starting handle at the front, which in its time had been credited with breaking at least one wrist and causing a sprain to many more, when the offending engine had failed to start first time.

On this occasion, as I hoped, the engine started readily. Belching out clouds of blue smoke which took some time to dissipate into the atmosphere, the noise level reduced to little more than a crescendo, due largely to the tractor shed being only a little larger than the tractor itself. I climbed into the driving seat and selected the reverse gear, which to my added relief, slipped in easily. I let out the clutch, reversed out of the shed and when clear, swung around to enable me to try out the three forward gears at full throttle up the green. I may well have driven it in reverse full throttle up the green as it was. I now had one reverse gear and only one forward, both of which enabled me to travel at about the same speed.

I hastily returned the tractor to the shed and dismantled it again, saying later, to a casual enquiry from Alfie, that "Yes I had fixed it, but it still needed a little adjustment which shouldn't take more than another day".

It was not long before I was given the task of going to Chartres to collect some mail, which had been sent there overland, from Fox Bay. The reason that I had drawn the short straw was because the bulk of the mail was most likely to be for me. Although I was not looking forward to the idea, there was little point in protesting. It was well known that I was eager to get my mail, the first news of home since my arrival.

The arrangement was that I would travel to Gun Hill shanty one afternoon, spend the night there and complete the rest of the journey the next day. The Chartres Manager having been told of my plans by radio, an important factor not to be overlooked, in order for someone in the settlement to keep a lookout for a lone rider, in addition to making sure that I was safe, it was the signal to send the boat over with the mail.

The principal reason for my reluctance to collect the mail had been that I had only travelled that way once before, when I first arrived and consequently I was unsure of the route, fortunately I had always been able to maintain a keen sense of direction. To my disadvantage was the need to take two horses again, for the extra load on the return journey and I was still a most inexperienced rider.

Although the ground underfoot was still dry it was getting well into winter and nightfall came quickly. That being the case, my plans had to include being at Gun Hill by 3.30 in the afternoon at the latest. I lost sight of the track many times but, by keeping an eye on the gap in the ridge, on the west side of the Narrows I was able to head generally in the right direction. Once through the Narrows I was able to pick up the coastline that led on into Christmas Harbour and the Chartres settlement, knowing that the shanty was on the beach, at a point where a small freshwater stream met the sea, so that even if I were to find myself too far in land, I would be able to pick up that stream closer to its source and follow it down to the beach.

The most difficult part of the journey was having to travel through Town Point, a long finger-like peninsula that jutted out into the channel that separated us from the Hill Cove camp to the North. Town Point was fenced off from the rest of the camp to prevent sheep from going into the near-white sand dunes where the wind quickly wiped out any sign of tracks to follow. It was simply a case of taking sight of landmarks and allowing them to be my guide.

I had taken with me, in addition to the two horses, Two-bob's old dog, Moss. He was very old but good company. Bill Paice had thought it a good idea for me to take him, secretly thinking that if I did somehow get lost the old dog would make his way back to the settlement. They would then know that they had to come looking for me. Fortunately that need never arose.

I arrived at the shanty as it was getting dark and with measurable relief, although apprehensive, the reason being that this was to be the first time that I had ever spent a night in a house on my own, or in this case a shanty, with Old Brock lying, supposedly, just a few yards away. My apprehension, for that reason, was something I had chosen to keep to myself.

The Chartres settlement was still an hour's ride away, even then the river separated us. It clearly would have been of little value to shout for help should I get into difficulty. I found that the absence of communication between people was something that we could, to some extent influence, but the total absence of people created a feeling of loneliness and extreme isolation.

I had no intention of venturing out after nightfall, so in order to avoid that ordeal, I hurriedly filled the peat buckets and topped up the oil lamp to ensure that there was sufficient to last the night. I did not mind turning the light down low but I was had no intention of turning it out altogether.

I ate the cold mutton and bread that I had brought with me, making sure that my intake of fluid was kept to a minimum. The same principal was applied to Moss. His advancing years may have induced bladder retention problems that could have required us to venture outside, I was not sure that I was ready for that.

With hindsight, in the clear light of day, it was all laughable. The night passed without incident, other than Moss having to make one night time visit which I was able to supervise from the doorway. The dawn was a welcome sight, as frequently was the case, with a clear sky and calm sea.

The small billowing white clouds against a background of pale blue sky created a scene of tranquillity. The only sound was that of the sea lapping gently on the beach. The wind would rise with the sun, but at that moment it was a world away and played no part in bringing to the beholder, "That peace that passes all understanding". It was difficult to appreciate that before we could have quietness we must have the absence of noise, any noise. We frequently found it in the early morning or late evening.

I left one of my horses at Gun Hill to be collected on the way back, then rode the remaining five miles to Chartres Point with the intention of arriving there about 9.30, in the hope that someone would be keeping a sharp lookout. As I entered the valley, at the Point, I saw movement on the jetty over the other side of the river and heard the motor-boat start up. To my relief that part of my purpose for being there had worked.

Jimmy Duncan manoeuvred the boat close into the shore and with the help of "Daggy" Hayward, with whom I had been at school some years before, put ashore two large sacks of mail, most of which, it transpired, was clothing purchased through the mail order catalogues, and not, after all, for me.

Mail order catalogues were a convenient way for Falkland Island families to purchase their clothing and household furnishings. The stores in Stanley were able to supply most things but the opportunity to view and select new styles was difficult for camp residents, although most families had friends or relatives living in Stanley, able to choose and purchase for them.

My nomination to collect the mail was also justified. There was a number of letters for me, but there was also a few hours riding ahead of me before I could settle down to read them.

Making sure that the mail was secure proved somewhat difficult, having left one horse at Gun Hill I had the double problem of not only securing the mail, I also had to leave sufficient room on top for me. The journey back was without incident. It was a fine day although, as I had predicted earlier, the wind had increased. I seemed to grow in confidence with each mile. The steep Devil Steps into the Narrows proved the most difficult. My inexperience was showing through, but I soon learnt that the horses found it much easier and consequently were more willing to travel up hill rather than down.

The arrival of mail into any settlement was greeted with great excitement. Letters from families and friends sometimes arrived three months after they were written and were carefully scrutinised to ensure that they were read in the right order, even then there were occasions when the sequel to family news arrived before the letter telling of the start. Such was the inconsistency of the postal system when distance, coupled with travel by land, sea and air, all had a part to play.

Newspapers from home travelled by surface mail and consequently arrived about three months after the date of publication. Like letters they rarely arrived singly.

The time between posting and delivery was equally unpredictable, Airmail letters rarely arrived within three weeks of posting due largely to the essential sea voyage between Montevideo and Stanley. Once mail arrived in the Colony it was sorted and despatched to its rightful destination as quickly as possible by sea, sometimes overland by horseback, tractor, or air. From one settlement to another. Mail carried by air or sea took second place to the real purpose of the journey.

One such occasion was when, under the auspices of the Falkland Government, an ambitious campaign was mounted to offer every resident of the islands a chest x-ray, similar to that made in the United Kingdom in the fight against tuberculosis. With its 1,800 or so residents scattered over 4,600 square miles, it presented quite a challenge. X-ray equipment was installed on board the *Philomel* and a small team of technicians under the leadership of a young German doctor embarked upon their mission, which took eighteen months to complete. With it came a quite happy coincidence. Like all forms of transport, the *Philomel* carried mail and small quantities of stores required by neighbouring farms, as it moved around the camp stations. This time, having carried out x-rays in Fox Bay and proposing to come to Dunnose Head for the same reason just two days later, it picked up surface mail from home for delivery to us at the same time. The *Philomel* had two bags of mail for us which was much more than usual, with many hands to help sort it. Most of it was mine, parcels, letters, cards, they were all there. The coincidence was there too. Eight thousand miles, three months travelling time, and it arrived that day of all days, my twenty first birthday!

Peter March joined us about this time, after a short, but enforced holiday in Stanley, somewhat in disgrace. He had been working as cook in Fox Bay West, but one of his-all-too-frequent pranks had resulted in him being "asked to leave!"

The final straw had come when he and a colleague, Noel Poole, attempted to bring the season's sheep work to a hasty conclusion, by draining the sheep dip before the final thousand sheep had passed through it. The problem had come to a head because the timing of the misdeed had coincided with an unusually dry summer which had reduced the freshwater streams to a trickle, leaving insufficient water to fill the dip, without which the remaining sheep would have to be slaughtered. The hasty departure was accompanied with a promise that, if the absence of rain resulted in the sheep having to be killed, he and Noel were going to have to pay for them and at about ten shillings each, they were not looking forward to that happening. When a spell of heavy and prolonged rain fell on Fox Bay he showed signs of being much relieved. Standing in front of the window, shouting "Rain you ****, rain".

Gun Hill Shanty.

CHAPTER 7

WINTER HOLIDAYS

Travelling during the winter months was never a pleasant experience. The inevitable driving rain, propelled by the seemingly never-ending gale force winds, helped to ensure that we were never totally comfortable. The essential heavy oilskin clothing rarely enabled the wearer to remain totally dry. In winter the low ground was waterlogged, which left the horses labouring fetlock deep in muddy peat. With farms some seven or nine hours ride apart, it was essential to take two horses, riding one about half of the intended distance before changing to the other, which, with the associated difficulties of having to lead the second horse, added to the general discomfort. It was often easier to tie the lead rein to the saddle of the horse we were riding: that also had its problems. Many riders could testify having had the saddle whipped from beneath them when the horse being led chose not to follow the lead horse after it had jumped a small stream.

The one or two roomed shanties, conveniently sited to provide a resting place for hard-working gangs of men during the busiest times of the year, of course were available for the traveller, if he wished to rest for the night. Most, however, preferred to press on and get to the journey's end. When left to men and horses, not all well made plans and intentions were successfully accomplished.

By tradition, the first week in July on the West Falklands was an annual holiday. Alfie and I decided to go to Fox Bay for the week, in spite of it being winter time, very wet and the added disadvantage of an eight hour horse ride.

Our preferred route on this occasion was a new one to me and took in the Narrows, Dog Hill, East Bay, Fox Bay West and finally around the harbour to Fox Bay East. An early start was important, if not essential; at best we would only have eight hours of daylight. Alfie had a scant knowledge of the route, I, of course, had none at all, just a general idea of the direction in which we were to go and that would have no value after dark, or if the day were to be one of low cloud and poor visibility. There were always gates to find, streams to cross, horse tracks to watch for as, more often than not, visual tracks were obliterated by wandering sheep.

Our early start failed to materialise. Alfie insisted on waiting for Bill to come and open the store so that he could take a bottle of whisky with him to keep out the cold, a requirement that included trying it out before we left which, as I was to learn, was a prelude to disaster.

It was eleven o'clock by the time we got away from the cookhouse and already starting to rain. We had barely left the settlement when we encountered our first obstacle, that of not being able to find our way out of the horse paddock. The difficulty was only to be overcome after we had ridden half a mile in either direction. Looking for the gate, the first two hours were beset with problems with regular stops to check the riding gear on our horses. This invariably meant that Alfie had to check the level of his whisky, which was already showing signs of decreasing and coincided with an increased inability on Alfie's part to co-ordinate both mentally and physically, although he appeared alert enough as he tried hard not to let me see him having a nip, by making sure that one of the horses obscured my view of him as he tipped up the bottle.

We went through the Narrows at about two o'clock and taking a brisk canter across the East Bay sands, we soon arrived at East Bay House, which was empty and unlocked. We concluded that its tenant, one of my former travelling companions, Geordie Douglas, also had decided to go into the settlement for a few days. We considered staying the night, as with hindsight we should have done, but Alfie assured me that we were within an hour or so's ride of the Fox Bay West settlement and should therefore press on and, being very much in his hands, I reluctantly agreed.

The rain became heavier as we headed out into the gathering dusk of the late afternoon and with it came an increasing reluctance on the part of the horses to trot on without persistent encouragement in the form of regular slaps with the bullock hide lead rein, coiled in the hand, as well as a dig from both heels into the flanks.

By this time, Alfie had consumed most of his "propelling fluid" and was showing a singular lack of interest in where we were going. The problem came to a head quite suddenly, when the horse that he was sitting on - it would have been wrong to say he was riding it - put its head down to have a drink from a small stream that came down from the hill to the north of us. In so doing, Alfie was pulled forward in the saddle and was unable to regain his balance in time to prevent himself from rolling down the horse's neck, fortunately becoming disentangled from his stirrups as he went, landed right in the stream. It was the last straw after a very difficult day, I felt no compunction to do anything other than leave him where he fell.

Catching all four horses, I removed the gear from the two that we had been riding and secured them as best as I could, the absence of trees taking on a greater significance. We had two hobblers which I placed on the legs of Alfie's horses, ensuring that they were able to move around but with their front legs strapped together they would be unable to travel far and, more long lead reins to the saddle which I proposed using as a pillow. It was going to be a long night, something like fifteen hours in all.

I had no real idea of the time, just that I was cold and wet. Alfie was possibly the same, but sympathy was not something I had in great abundance at that time. While I had been securing the horses he had managed to drag himself out of the stream, but still showed signs of feeling little pain and as I was past caring for his well being, I left him to get wetter and colder. For me, it was the oilskins that I was wearing, the horse blankets and anything I could find to offer me some protection.

After some hours the rain stopped. As the skies cleared, it became colder. The moon shone through the fast moving clouds. At least things did not look quite so hopeless, although I was conscious of the wet beneath me seeping through the blankets and it was still a long time from dawn. The horses remained tethered to the saddle and their presence made sure that I did not sleep for too long at a time. When their curiosity got the better of them they would nuzzle close, their hot breath on my face waking me with a start, while Alfie slept on oblivious to the cold or the horses.

When in Stanley, before going out to Fox Bay, I had bought a pair of steel stirrups with a five inch tread. I was using them on this particular occasion and they were also to be instrumental in my next lesson about horses. I had no idea how long I had been asleep, but it was certainly long enough for it to become deep and relaxed, when something caused me to wake with a such a start that I sat up quickly, momentarily wondering where I was. My sudden action caused the horses to jerk back in fright and in doing so pulled the saddle out from under me, resulting in the stirrups clanging together and frightening them even more. The end result was that they bolted into the darkness.

The commotion awoke Alfie who lurched to his feet, not even sure which day of the week it was, clearly unable to understand why he was able to hear the sound of bells ringing in the distance.

We were able to track the horses by the sound as they cantered in a complete circle around us. When they eventually stopped I made my way to where I had last heard them, stumbling and falling in the darkness as I made my way through the fachine bushes. Twice the sound of my noisy approach frightened them into cantering off, the stirrups ringing out into the night. Eventually I was able to get close enough to untie them from the saddle and lead them back to where Alfie was waiting with the rest of our riding gear. It was clear that the effects of the whisky had largely worn off but the residual effects were very much in evidence. He stood, wet and cold, shivering from head to toe, unable to stop shaking long enough to roll himself a cigarette. His whisky had long since run out, and I was still far from pleased at what I saw to be his fault and the subject of our predicament, but I succumbed to his plea to roll him a cigarette, which had only limited success. I, too, was cold and not at all experienced at rolling cigarettes but at that moment to him it was like breath to a dying man. It was still too dark to attempt to find our way into Fox Bay West so we lay down as best we could to await the dawn of another day. This time firmly holding on to the lead reins and I vowed never to tie a horse to the front of a saddle again.

Fitful sleep came in spells of two or three minutes at a time when the exhaustion fought through the cold and discomfort, until there was sufficient light to enable us to saddle up and head for Fox Bay. The West Head now clearly visible on the horizon although still some way off. So much, I thought, for Alfie's estimate the night before that Fox Bay West was only an hour's ride away. It was exactly twenty four hours since leaving Dunnose Head before we were able to get on the best side of a most welcome cup of coffee, we still had an hour's ride around the harbour to Fox Bay East. We were however, safe and nearly sound. An experience I had no wish to repeat but pleased to have had it now that it was over.

As we rode along we discussed tactics and made the decision not to reveal the fact that we had been out all night. The idea had been Alfie's, not wishing to have the embarrassment of explaining, to all who asked, how it came about, coming so quickly after his encounter with Mr Clements at the Hawks Nest shanty. We had, of course, been expected the previous night, but as usual the assumption had been made that we had spent the night at East Bay House and that was the story that Alfie was happy for people to believe. In my innocence, yet again, by agreeing with him, I was shortly to make another mistake.

Our visit coincided with that of Robert Stout, brother of the Fox Bay East cook Jim Stout. Robert was working at Port Howard to the north and had been prompted to make the visit by the need for someone to collect the mail, delivered to Fox Bay some days earlier. Robert, like many of his contempories, enjoyed a drink, often it seemed, to excess. Indeed Robert was in the habit of preparing for any eventuality by arming himself with as many bottles of spirits as he thought necessary to see him through the week. With a two gallon bucket to go under the bed, he would then repair to his room, there to stay until the bottles were empty and the bucket full. His waking periods were used solely for the purpose of transferring fluid from the bottle to himself and from himself to the bucket. On this occasion and towards the end of the week, the peace was shattered by a commotion in the region of the cookhouse stairs. There was a rush to open the door only to find Robert, dripping wet, clutching a now empty bucket. The noise and his reclined position clearly indicating that he had fallen from top to bottom. Brother Jim broke the silence that followed by asking, "What are you doing down here Robert?" which prompted the slow and, carefully considered reply, "I only came down to collect the mail".

Alfie's brother, Don Banks, also had travelled from Port Howard for the holiday. He arrived mid-way through the week looking much the worse to bottom. Brother Jim broke the silence that followed by asking, "What are you doing down here Robert?" which prompted the slow and, carefully considered reply, "I only came down to collect the mail".

Alfie's brother, Don Banks, also had travelled from Port Howard for the holiday. He arrived mid-way through the week looking much the worse for wear, his balding head and nose scarred and bleeding from a recent encounter with the ground. With history and local knowledge indicating that his injuries had been sustained through over-indulgence, he steadfastly maintained that he had been unfortunate enough to have been thrown from his horse and, while unconscious, had been attacked by seagulls, hence the scars. His version of events fell on deaf ears, somewhere we had heard it all before.

At the end of our holiday and shortly before leaving for Dunnose Head, it became clear that Alfie had unintentionally, but quite effectively, put me in a position of some embarrassment. Fortified by more than one good measure of strong refreshment, he had told the truth about our night out under the stars, while I was still upholding our agreed story that it had been spent at East Bay House, which was sufficient reason for me, whenever in collusion with Alfie, to tell the truth right from the start, as a secret lasted no longer than the next trip to the store.

About a month after our winter holiday I developed toothache which was sufficiently painful to require me to return to Fox Bay for medical attention. The doctor was not in the habit of dealing with dentistry matters, but at the time the islands were without a camp dentist.

Had there been one, his responsibility would have included travelling around the various farms, spending a few weeks at each one, dealing with fillings and extractions.

to find a patient, who wished to object.

Having administered the anaesthetic, the dentist would set up his surgery outside the cookhouse, have his patients stand in a line, then one by one, he would approach them from behind, place a firm grip around the neck and leaning over the shoulder remove the offending tooth with one sharp downward pull of the forceps.

Another occasion when the comforts of the dentist's chair were sadly lacking was the time the dentist was required to attend a patient on one of the smaller islands. He was flown out in an Auster, one of the earliest aircraft operated by the Falkland Island Government Air Service. The plane landed in the harbour, close to the settlement. However the wind was quite strong and according to the weather report, was going to get steadily worse, which forced the need to get airborne and back to Stanley as quickly as possible. It was arranged by radio, before the aircraft landed, that the patient would be ferried out to the aircraft as soon as it landed. There, bobbing up and down in the heavy swell, the dentist removed the offending tooth, barely allowing time for the anaesthetic to take effect, and the Auster then took off with the utmost speed to the relief of both the dentist and the patient.

Two-bob Skilling never seemed to suffer from toothache, not necessarily due to the fact that he had very few teeth. Those that did remain were right in the front and very loose, so loose that he developed the extremely aggravating habit of moving them back and forwards with his tongue.

With the absence of electric light, it was usual to move between the different rooms in the cookhouse without the aid of a light, which greatly assisted the advancement of practical jokes. A usual one was to run a length of fine thread across the hallway and stairs, thereby causing anger and upset to unsuspecting colleagues who had the misfortune to walk into it. One such occasion caused Tom to lose both of his coveted front teeth when the unseen outstretched thread went into his mouth and, taken aback by the surprise encounter, he jerked his head back suddenly and in so doing removed them both.

Needless to say he was very upset. No amount of reassurance or reminder of how much less painful it was than a trip to the dentist consoled him. He seemed more upset at the loss of something to wobble with his tongue than the actual loss of his teeth.

Nevertheless, I needed no reassurance that my toothache was going to disappear with far less trouble as I settled down in the Doctor's surgery armchair. The doctor, Geoffrey Greenaway, was also a newcomer to the Falklands. It was only as we chatted, while waiting for the anaesthetic to take effect, that he let it slip that he had never had either the opportunity or the inclination to extract a tooth before and was only doing so now through lack of choice.

Whether inevitably, or due to being over-cautious, we never knew, but the tooth disintegrated under the pressure of his grip on the forceps which caused him to enter a state of some agitation, fearful that once the anaesthetic wore off I would be subjected to some considerable pain, sufficient for me to be flown to Stanley for treatment at the hospital.

64

CHAPTER 8

THE COLOURFUL COOK

During the long winter evenings at Dunnose Head, Peter March recounted many of the escapades that he had become involved in, always it seemed with him ending up as the hero and some unsuspecting colleague as the villain. One such occasion had been when he was working as cook at Fox Bay West.

The Station Manager, Charlie Robertson, had visited the cookhouse before breakfast one morning, to see a member of the gang who was supposedly sick. He went straight up the stairs, pausing just long enough to place his trilby hat on the long, freshly scrubbed table. Peter, for reasons best known to himself, seized the opportunity to spread a very generous helping of golden syrup around the brim of his Boss's hat. On his return Mr.Robertson duly replaced his hat on his head and made to leave, exactly as Peter had anticipated, but having reached the doorway, he stopped and turned to talk to him instead. The warmth of the day and that from Mr Charlie's head caused the syrup to gently trickle down the side of his face. Once or twice he made to brush away the irritation. On about the third occasion, he realised that it was sticky and took off his hat while Peter, projecting a picture of innocence, looked on enquiringly. This distracted Mr. Robertson from his original thought of who was the most likely candidate to have put golden syrup around the brim of his hat, vowing, as he finally left, that if Peter could find out who had done such a thing he would do his best to make sure that the culprit never forgot that syrup was intended to be spread on toast, not around his bloody hat.

On another occasion, shortly after turn-to time, Mr. Robertson again visited the cookhouse, this time accompanied by the doctor who had been brought across the harbour from Fox Bay East by his guide, Chris Perry. Peter was in the galley, preparing breakfast for the gang, who were already busy at work in the shearing shed. When the visitors arrived they went straight upstairs where they remained for some time. When he heard footsteps coming down the stairs Peter went to see what the "to-do" was all about. Seeing the doctor, he said: "Hello, Who's sick then?" which prompted Mr. Robertson to give the snap reply, "Who's sick? Who's dead you mean!", and the party went upon its way. Peter, in two short strides, bounded up the stairs and headed straight for the room of a colleague who he knew to have been a little unwell the previous day. In his cheery laughing manner, he said "Old Charlie told me you were dea...?" He never finished what he was going to say, but beat a hasty retreat, for dead the patient surely was.

Peter was capable of turning his hand to many things, but his greatest interest seemed to be in cooking, perhaps because, as cook, he would not have to get too involved with the sheep work, or because he was able to avoid working outside in the worst of the weather. Most certainly, his interest in cooking should never have been taken as an implied ability to cook well. It couldn't be denied that he was an adventurous cook, always prepared to try something that little bit different.

Biscuits were his speciality, particularly in terms of quantity, the quality was perhaps a different story. Regardless of the recipe employed, there was always one dominant characteristic present in them all. They were always hard. A durability test was applied to one of his infamous diamond shaped biscuits that somehow found its way out to Shallow Harbour. The test was perhaps unintentional, but nevertheless effective. The biscuit in question was nailed, for purely decorative purposes, to the front door of the house and stayed there for some months, enduring an entire winter, before receiving two coats of paint, which only served to ensure its place in history as the only door in the islands whose decoration had started out in life by being offered up for human consumption.

It was for his colourful presentations that Peter was best remembered. Numerous colours were employed in the making of sponge cakes. Invariably in bright colours, with pink, blue and green being those most likely to attract his attention.

During one of his low periods, while still working at Fox Bay West, criticism was made, by more than one of his colleagues, that his meals were lacking in variety and imagination. This cutting remark had the immediate effect of hurting his feelings. Not being one to sulk about such remarks, he made up his mind to make amends and thereby avoid being the subject of such cruelty ever again. The chosen method he kept very much to himself until a few days later when the gang was all sitting around the table, eagerly awaiting lunch. Peter brought in two roasting pans each containing a large roast of mutton, gravy and onions. He placed them on the centre of the table and returned to the galley, only to emerge a few seconds later with four rather thickly sliced loaves of bread, one brown, one blue, one green and yes, one pink. Criticisms, particularly of the cook, never failed to tempt providence, only the simple-minded would attempt it a second time.

The cook was not required to provide meals in the cookhouse at the weekend, only to make sure that there was sufficient cooked, cold meat available, plus a few loaves of bread. We were very fortunate that our cook at Dunnose Head was an exception to the rule, he invariably made a small fruit cake for "Smoko" on Sunday morning and we also had a hot lunch.

"Two-bob" Skilling was a big man and gave the impression that he was rolling rather than walking. He was unable to read or write and had gained his nickname from the price that he put on everything, whether buying or selling. Although a widower, he had a lady acquaintance in Stanley with whom he corresponded both rarely and briefly. Apart from calling on her during his infrequent visits to town, his only other contact was via a Christmas Greeting telegram transmitted over the radio network which, if Tom had his way, was no more than "Merry Christmas, Tom". Much prompting was required before he would say "Alright then , Merry Christmas, Love, Tom".

There were only four of us to cater for: Alfie, Peter, yours truly and Tom himself. The cookhouse was small with three single rooms upstairs. Downstairs there was Tom's bedroom, the galley and mess, side by side with an interconnecting door by the sink and drainer, from where Tom could look out of the window and make incorrect predictions about what the weather was going to do next. Incorrect because the prevailing winds invariably ensured that the clouds he was looking at had passed over our heads some time before and were going the other way.

Both the mess and the galley had a separate entrance, each protected by a small porch where, in Tom's case, he kept his peat buckets ready for when he wanted them.

In Dunnose Head we had a small but special stud flock. Four rams had been imported from New Zealand at great expense, to breed with the special flock and in doing so improve the quality of the wool, a necessary requirement from time to time. The rams were quite impressive; short, stocky build, with neatly curled horns. In order to keep them in tip-top condition they were allowed to roam around the enclosure, in which the cookhouse stood, when not running with the ewes.

One day Alfie thought that life was far too peaceful and needed to be livened up, so with much puffing and pulling we caught one of the rams and put a hessian sack over its head. Then, as quietly as we could under the circumstances, shut it in Tom's dark porch, the darkness ensuring that it would stay quiet, at least until something gave it reason to do otherwise.

With laudable pretence of total innocence, we waited patiently until Tom picked up two empty buckets from beside the range and made for the peat stack, which was about fifty feet from his porch door. On cue, as we had predicted, when Tom opened the galley door, that led into the porch, the ram, having seen a chink of daylight for the first time since it was shut in, charged. With a roar from the cook, a muffled bleat from the ram and a crash of peat buckets, everything that was not either nailed or screwed down took to the air: pots, pans, plates and the cook. The ram got into the pantry and mixed the coffee, which came in six pound bags, with a 56 pound bag of flour. Pandemonium reigned for what seemed like an age, but was in fact just a matter of minutes. In any event it would have been very difficult to plan such a scene of devastation.

Tom took some time to overcome his part of the ordeal, reminding us frequently just how close he had come to having a serious collapse of the respiratory system due to an excessive intake of coffee-flavoured flour.

It was rare for Tom to venture far from the settlement, apart from his infrequent three months' winter holiday in Stanley. He would occasionally pay a weekend visit to the outside shepherd, Norman Henrickson, at

Shallow Harbour. Even then he would only go if we were willing to take part in the preparations. That involved us catching his horse, putting on the saddle and reins, then assisting him to get on, which could only be achieved by finding a low bank where the sheep had worn away much of the top soil, thereby enabling us to get the horse in close. With its back at almost ground level, it was possible for Tom to do little more than step on. Even then, when the time for him to leave got close he would start to make excuses, generally by standing in the interconnecting doorway between the galley and mess, looking out of the window and making more outrageous weather forecasts. It was a ritual that we had to endure regardless of the infrequency of his visits.

On one particular weekend the boot was on the other foot. He was having difficulty in getting someone to go out into the paddock and catch his horse. An earlier decision had been made that he would take Cleo an elderly, slow but reliable white mare. Reliable in the sense that once caught and geared up, she would stand and wait, the rest of the day if necessary, for her rider to get on. All sorts of requests and threats had been made to no avail. Only when Tom threatened to evoke cook's rights and withdraw hot meals on Sundays, did Alfie give in, mumbling under his breath, as he went to catch the horse, that, "If it's horse he wants, it's horse he's going to get".

Tom went to his room to get ready, which called for a clean white collarless shirt, grey suit, trousers tucked into turned-down Wellington boots, blue beret pulled well down over one ear and a blue flowered silk scarf tied loosely around his neck. All this took time, more than enough in fact, for Alfie to catch Cleo and bring her into the enclosure around the cookhouse, but that was not enough. Tom was still in his room when Alfie led the horse in through the porch and into the galley. That was something that could not be done quietly, a one ton horse with four feet, each the size of dinner plates, making slow and deliberate clomp, clomp, clomp, noises brought Tom from his room. Usually, under such circumstances, he would have asked what the hell was going on, but this time he could see for himself, consequently he launched into a string of uncomplimentary words, all aimed at Alfie and designed to bring into question both his sanity and parentage.

The commotion and the sound of its own feet on the hollow wooden floor was, to say the least, making Cleo nervous and it was possibly that same nervousness that caused Tom, who noticed it first, primarily because he was at that end, to shout, with other things, "Get it out, it's lifting tail".

Hot, steaming, rhubarb-growing agent is not generally attractive to the sense of smell and that was true on this occasion. Pull and coax as he did Alfie was unable to turn Cleo around in the close confines of the galley, it was not easy getting a fully grown horse through a two foot six inch doorway. When he eventually got her out, Tom took up from where he had left off, seemingly in awe of the volume of fresh fertiliser that had been deposited throughout the two downstairs rooms of the cookhouse.

Alfie began to question the wisdom of his latest escapade when he ventured back into the cookhouse to clear up, which he attempted to do in a series of short quick trips, his only tools being a small brush and dustpan. The lingering smell was obviously getting through to his senses, as, standing some twenty feet from the open doorway, he could be heard retching violently. which alternated with obscene utterances aimed at those who had actively supported the original intention of helping a colleague spend a quiet weekend with friends and were now disassociating themselves entirely from the result, other than pointing the way to the kitchen garden.

CHAPTER 9

NICK'S WINTER MIXTURE

The transition between seasons, particularly in winter and spring, came slowly. Nevertheless even in the shortest periods of daylight, we were able to keep busy with jobs that enabled us to keep dry, with perhaps only two or three days during the entire year when we were obliged to abandon work altogether and stay in the cookhouse. These stays were always to the consternation of the cook who protested that he was the only one required to keep working on the entire farm. An attitude reminiscent of our schooldays when mother complained that we were always under her feet during the extended school holidays.

One essential task during the winter, come rain, storm or sunshine, was to cut tussock grass for the milking cows. More than one storm-tossed boat made its way to an offshore island with some trepidation to return loaded to the gunwales with perhaps fifty or sixty sheaves of tussock grass, each weighing about fifty pounds.

For the shepherd, living an hour's ride or sometimes two, from the settlement, it was quite different. With few outbuildings to maintain, he would stay close to home during the worst of the winter storms and a period of two or three weeks could elapse before he considered it prudent or beneficial to venture out into the camp to check on selected flocks of sheep. The most important, of course, were the ewes who towards the end of winter were heavily in lamb. The possibility of wool around the face and eyes, obscuring clear vision, combined to place them in danger of falling into the swollen streams. His job in such cases was to take them further inland and on to higher ground.

It was unusual for the shepherd to come into the settlement during the winter months other than to get additional stores. It seemed that the only other time that we saw Norman Henrickson was when one of his dogs decided to make a bid for freedom from her kennel and go looking for a boy friend, invariably to be found in the settlement. It happened so frequently that Norman gave firm instructions that we were to catch her and shut her in one of our kennels until such times as he was able to collect her, something that he was reluctant to do, mainly because of the frequency of the event. Apart from the difficulties associated with trying to catch her, it also caused Alfie's dog, Nick considerable anguish and frustration. After two break-outs in little more than a week, we hit on an idea that had never been very far from our thoughts, an idea that would keep most of us happy, Nick, we felt sure, would be more than pleased, even very willing, to play his part. Norman's dog would be happy to stay with its master at Shallow Harbour and Norman would be relieved of the chore of having a two hour return journey to collect her. The end result was that one and one made five nice little black and white puppies, with just the slightest hint of brown, that caused just one finger of suspicion to be pointed at Nick.

Those of us with rather more detailed knowledge of events could only look in wonder and surprise when Nick seemed like getting the blame, perhaps more than a little hurt at the implied suggestion that we had failed in our responsibility towards a colleague and his dog, while Nick showed signs of total indifference when his name came up in casual conversation.

From time to time Peter and I went out to Shallow Harbour to spend the weekend with Norman, his wife Iris and their two small daughters.

Iris disliked living so far away from the settlement and people, with no one other than the family to talk to so it was with particular eagerness that we were made welcome. We would plan to arrive in the early afternoon on Saturday to be greeted by Norman saying, "I'm glad you arrived early, I wonder if you would just give me a hand to fix the gate into the cowshed", or some other task that had somehow just arisen. Some months and a number of visits elapsed before Tommy Skilling let it slip, just before an intended visit, that Norman had a store of tasks lined up for Peter and I to help him with. Preferring, it seemed, to keep us working outside as long as possible and not enjoying the company of his wife indoors.

The purpose of the visit as far as Peter and I were concerned was abundantly clear. There was the welcome respite from the endless round of cookhouse meals for one thing, but more to the point and, very much in our thoughts when making the decision to go to Shallow Harbour, was the prospects of having a late night feast of waffles and fresh cream. That was invariably the highpoint of our weekend.

It was usually the womenfolk who looked after the cows and made sure that they were milked regularly, generally easy enough in the settlements where the cowshed, corral and paddock fences were well maintained. However, for the shepherds, particularly the single ones, much was left to chance and the good nature of the cows. Hence, fresh milk was rarely plentiful and the by-products of cream and butter largely unavailable, certainly during the long autumn and winter. The fences, primarily erected to contain the sheep, were no match for the cow that was determined to go in search of fresh grass and vegetation. Once loose, her absence often stretched into days before she could be found and brought back home again, only to have a repeat performance a few days later.

Fortunately for the family man with well maintained fences, only one cow was required to keep his family in fresh milk. Any left over could be put in a bottle and placed in nature's own cooler, the cool and crystal clear water of the natural spring or stream that was invariably found close to the house, from where he would get the water for domestic use.

There was, however, one regular obstacle in our way at Shallow Harbour before we could think about warming the waffle iron. Norman had one cow that was a particular favourite, mainly because she was very tame and content to stay close to the house, but also because she provided all the milk required for his family.

The other cows were allowed to run with their calves, who were, in turn, more than willing to suckle their parent even at eight or nine months old, or until such times that the cow had another calf.

Notwithstanding the fact that Norman's old cow was a good milker, it was still not enough to keep us in nice, thick cream, to heap on freshly made waffles, so an additional supply of fresh milk was required. We needed little convincing that Norman's "First reserve" cow was both headstrong and a trifle wild, so much so that more often than not the three of us were required to extract what the cow clearly saw as the forbidden fruit. Having got her within the corral that surrounded the cowshed, the next task was to get close enough to place a rope around her horns. Contrary to popular belief, using a lasso was not second nature to a cowboy. Our ploy, and the one that proved for us to be the most successful, was for one of us to perch somewhat precariously on top of the high fence with a length of coiled rope, looped at one end, ready to drop it over the horns of the reluctant cow as she   charged by, hotly pursued by the other two would-be mil-kmen. After several attempts, the "securing one unhappy cow" part of the mission was completed. The rest had to be easier but no one had yet written a fail-safe manual on how to secure and milk a cow. The head of our particular cow was tied in tight and close to the ground, making sure that she was unable to move either backwards or forwards. To prevent lateral movement two of us were required to keep her pinned, as best they could, close into the wall of the cowshed while the third, with much fear and justifiable trepidation, pulled gently on the teats that contained the milk, a move guaranteed not to calm the anxious animal.

Driven on by the desire not to be beaten, it would take as much as an hour from the moment we entered the corral until it was generally agreed that we had a sufficient quantity, of the hard won substance for our needs, by which time we were almost too exhausted to separate the cream from the milk, in preparation for our long awaited treat. The simple pleasures of life, so readily available at home, seemed impossibly hard to obtain. It was always well into the night before we had our fill of waffles and cream, the time between the almost constant round of cooking and eating, in the absence of any outside distraction, was spent telling tales of unfortunate happenings to absent friends and of home, which, at times seemed a million miles away and a distance never to be bridged.

SHALLOW HARBOUR

CHAPTER 10

DOWN THE CLIFF FACE

When writing letters home, it was easy to create the impression that the weather, in comparison to that of the United Kingdom, was always bad. That was not so. It had to be admitted that the hostile elements of the South Atlantic gave rise to strong, frequently gale force, winds, which prevented trees becoming established, life on board small boats hazardous, and work outside unpleasant. Whatever the task, due consideration of the prevailing weather was always necessary. When erecting a new timber framed house it was important to remember to position it in such a way that a corner cut the prevailing wind, not to do so meant that the side of the building took the full force of the wind, risking it being lifted from its foundations.

Like all things endured for a period of time, they become common place and taken for granted to such an extent that their absence had an immediate effect on the usual routine. Such was the situation on calm winter nights, the absence of wind continually buffeting the building usually resulted in a sleepless night. It was simply too quiet. Some people look for soothing music to bring relaxation and sleep but there were those who preferred a keen fresh wind creating it own sounds. Equally the gales which lashed the area for days on end could cause extreme frustration and even anger when the simplest task, such as lighting a cigarette, keeping a beret on, or even walking upright proved impossible.

Perhaps less frequent, but far from unusual were those periods of memorable, quiet calm that had no comparison with the descriptions "God forsaken", "Inhospitable" and the implied derogatory term "The other end of the world" - all at some time used to describe the islands. All untrue, they failed completely to reflect the beauty and peace that was all around. The creative power of a force beyond man's understanding could be seen in the hills, the deep sheltered valleys, the birds and marine life. The stillness itself when the water in the harbours reflected a quiet calm and its own natural beauty. So calm and still could be the water and air that even the slap of an oar on the water could be heard half a mile away and, as unbelievable as it may seem, on more than one occasion, while standing outside the cookhouse at Dunnose Head, I heard the highest notes of a cockerel crowing at Shallow Harbour, a distance of some four or five miles, echoing through the valley and around the hills. The contrast between the calm and the storm were often highlighted by the sound of the sea outside the sheltered harbour, crashing on the barren rocks around the coastline, while I stood in a motionless vacuum. With the lengthening days and the signs of spring all around, the arrival of the lambs heralded the start of a new season, when the shepherds day started at dawn and carried on until dusk.

The first day of November was always the day nominated to start lamb marking in Dunnose Head. The breeding ewes spent the winter months in a long peninsular leading down to Rous Creek. at the extreme westerly end of the farm, a two-hour horse ride from the settlement, or a further hour beyond Shallow Harbour. There was no accommodation at that end of the farm so it had been the practice at the end of a tiring day, to return to Shallow Harbour for the night. Consequently, a typical day started in the settlement at four o'clock in the morning and finished at eight or nine o'clock at night, leaving little time for eating or a restful sleep. Our plan this year, if achieved, was to end all that and make subsequent visits, work and sleeping arrangements much less demanding.

A prefabricated, single room shanty had been landed at the creek, by the New Island cutter, half a mile from the selected site. After the completion of lamb marking, we were going to stay on for a further three days and erect the shanty close to the sheep pens. Everything we needed was there, the timber frame, each piece cut and marked ready to fit together, galvanised sheeting for the roof and cladding for the outside walls, nails, screws, window and glass.

A day here or there would have little effect on our plans for the week, but it was agreed that Peter and I would travel to Rous Creek on the Sunday afternoon, taking the tractor and trailer, loaded with a nine-man bell tent, tools, and sufficient tinned food, cold meat and bread to keep us going for a week. Bill Paice, Alfie, Norman Henrickson and young George would join us about breakfast time on Monday morning, with additional horses for Peter and me. We would then be in a position to start the gather without any delay. The reason for taking the tent was that the journey would take much longer than on horseback as there was no recognised track for wheeled vehicles between the settlement and our destination, the ground was uneven, and there was a difficult little stream to cross at the foot of a valley, which led up to the house at Shallow Harbour.

Peter was keen to leave on Sunday morning. He wanted to take some photographs of the cliffs and of the gulls which we knew nested there, only two hundred yards from where we were going to pitch the tent. Consequently, we set out early, planning to have lunch at Shallow Harbour. The journey was slow and uncomfortable, but without incident, apart from when I drove the tractor over the narrow stream which had overhanging sides. The fast-running water had eroded the stream bed, creating a drop of about two feet. The bank gave way as I drove over it with the end result that the tractor jack-knifed, rear end first, vertically into the stream, taking with it the trailer drawbar. The trailer that had been four feet behind me suddenly came close to crushing me in the driving seat, as the drawbar and the tractor came together with a crash.

It was a narrow escape from a potentially serious accident, medical attention was at least ten hours horse ride away. Being Sunday the radio link with Stanley would not be in use and our nearest land line was at Chartres, at least five hours ride away. It was well not to reflect on what could have been.

We arrived at our final destination about two o'clock, with a thirty knot wind blowing and we had some difficulty in erecting the bell tent. At Peter's insistence, we left the remainder of the unpacking for later, he was fearful that there would be insufficient light left to take photographs.

We had brought with us a new coil of rope, two hundred feet in length, which Peter intended to use to support himself as he took some truly original photographs. I had never been that close to the edge of a cliff before and was quite prepared to forego the pleasure ever again. We were standing within two feet of the edge of nowhere with a gale force wind blowing in off the open sea, with below us a sheer drop of something like three hundred feet. Fortunately, the roar of the wind drowned out the sound of twenty feet high waves bursting onto the rocks below. The gulls, undoubtedly flying well above the waves, looked like tiny specks in the distance.

Standing there totally exposed to the elements did not impress me one tiny bit. To crown it all, Peter was expecting me to lower him over the edge on a rope. The fact that it was he who wanted to take the photographs, and it was he that was going over the edge, did nothing to mitigate my fears or apprehension. I had no love for heights under any circumstances and although I was standing on firm ground I still had the feeling that I was up very high, to leave this particular scene was very high on the list of my most earnest intentions.

Peter was uncomplimentary and unforgiving about my feelings. Over the noise of the wind, he explained what, with my help and undivided attention, we were going to do. The rope was tied around his waist, a coil around mine and the other end, at my insistence, tied around a metal stanchion which fortunately marked the end of a fence at the spot where Peter proposed, quite clearly, to place himself in incredible danger, with me, a devout coward, playing an active part.

He lowered himself over the edge, his camera hanging loosely around his neck. At no more than ten feet over the edge it was impossible to hear a word of what he was trying to say. The wind simply took away every word. Peter seemed to be insanely fearless. Letting go of the rope as he took shots with his camera from every angle, waving his arms frantically as he tried to indicate to me that he wanted more rope, to enable him to go lower.

When he reached an overhanging ledge of rock, about one hundred feet down the cliff face, I decided that enough was enough, inspite of his vigorous tugs on the rope, I refused to pay out any more line. Taking up the slack, I tied it firmly to the stanchion, determined that Peter was now going to come up, or at least he was not going to have my help in going down any further. Trying to communicate with him was quite pointless, the more I tugged on the rope as an indication that I wanted him to come up, the more he gestured to me that he wished to go down even further. Holding firmly onto the stanchion I cautiously allowed myself a look over the edge of the abyss. All I could see was Peter, feet pressed firmly into the cliff, from where he was projecting his body away from the face, taking photographs as he went. Later to be described as an uninterrupted view of the sea at its most savage, it was a point of view with which I could not disagree. Forced to come up because of my refusal to give him more line made Peter angry and upset and I was equal in my unrepentance. As if by way of an excuse, I said: "We still have work to do, unloading the trailer".

Peter was without fear, whether it be of man, horse or machine. He was an experienced colt tamer, but, as far as I was concerned, the fault lay in him failing to recognise that not everyone, particularly myself, displayed the same qualities.

With about an hour of daylight left after unloading the trailer and getting all of our belongings into the tent, we went to look for goose eggs in the long white grass just a short way from the tent. There was very little time to look for nests after a day's toil, once the sheep work got under way, so to find some now would ensure that we had some variety with the cold mutton that we had brought with us. We were successful in finding two nests, yielding about a dozen eggs and went back to the tent to eat and settle down for the night. The rest of the gang were expected soon after first light the next morning. We had with us a .22 calibre rifle with which we had hoped to get a goose for supper, but had overlooked the need to bring something to cook it in and, as a consequence, the idea had to be abandoned.

Although the wind was still blowing hard, we were comfortable in the tent. In the early evening we climbed into our sleeping bags and settled down for the night. Peter was in no mood for polite conversation. With just two of us, there was plenty of room and we were able to position ourselves on either side of the centre pole. By the light of a candle, pushed down inside an empty condensed milk tin, in which a hole had been made with two sharp blows from a sheath knife, we tried to read. One candle power proved insufficient and after a few minutes we did the best thing possible by snuggling right down into the sleeping bags and pulling the zips up high to try to shut out the noise of the wind.

It was only after we had got comfortable that the question arose as to who was going to put out the light? Neither it seemed, having got nicely settled, was prepared to move. Peter was still upset at my lack of co-operation earlier in the day. I tried to ignore the light and after a few minutes dozed off into a gentle sleep, only to be shaken back into consciousness by a dull thump originating from just a few feet away. I looked in the direction of the sound to see Peter, still lying in his sleeping bag, with the .22 rifle resting across his chest and, quite obviously without taking proper aim, trying to shoot the wick off the candle, with the result that small lumps of lead, more commonly known as bullets, were being projected across the tent, at x feet per second, between two and four inches above my prone body, making tiny little holes in the side of the canvas tent as they went upon their way. All this only served to confirm my belief that Peter was quite oblivious to danger but, unlike the afternoon's escapade, it was now me on the receiving end. I asked for an amnesty to be declared, while I sat up and blew out the candle.

We had a kettle boiling on a makeshift fire when Bill Paice and the boys arrived the next morning. They had already spent nearly three hours in the saddle and welcomed the cup of tea we offered them. As we sat in the tent talking about our drive down the day before, Bill's eye caught sight of some small holes in the canvas and asked if we had caught the tent on a nail, as there seemed to be a number of small tears in the side, about a foot off the ground. We could not recall seeing any nails and quickly changed the subject, suggesting that we should press on and gather the ewes and their lambs, if we were going to get any work done at all.

It was not unusual, or difficult, for me to get lost during a gather, as good eyesight was something that I did not have. The rider to your right or to the left, could be as much as half a mile away, and with dogs working between, we tried to ensure that all the sheep kept moving ahead. The wind played a big part in making sure that we had a clean gather. If the sheep were running into the wind, they would run ahead with comparative ease, the wind flattening the fleece to the body. Under those circumstances, the dogs would have little work to do, if the sheep were being driven forward, with the wind coming from behind, the story was quite different. The wind would then lift the fleece and make the sheep cold, which only served to encourage the animal to turn round and try to go the other way, or find a cluster of rocks behind which to hide. Consequently, the wind could determine if the gather was going to take two hours or three.

The lamb marking was completed in just over two days. The job involved bringing all the ewes and their lambs together at one point, driving them into large pens sufficient to hold up to 3,000 animals, then drive them all through a narrow race, with gates opening off on either side. As the sheep ran through, the gates were opened to allow the ewes to run back out to the camp. The lambs were ushered into large pens to await the ritual of castration for the ram lambs, with a rubber ring placed tightly over the scrotum, and similarly tail-docking, which helped to keep the sheep clean and prevent infection, and marks or tags were placed in the ears to identify the owner, age and sex of each one.

The sheep work finished, we got on with building the shanty. It did not take long to join together the numbered pieces of the timber frame, clad the outside and line the inside with thick sheets of plywood.

By Friday, five days after we had arrived, all that was left to do was to erect the small peat burning stove, before leaving for the settlement. The only task that we had been unable to complete was to fix the skirting-board that went around the edge of the floor, somehow it had been missed off the list of material supplied with the rest of the building.

Almost as an afterthought, we strung wires across the shanty on which to hang the skins of a dozen sheep that we had killed either to feed the dogs or because they were clearly unable to keep up the rest of the flock and, knowing that we would be returning to Rous Creek in a matter of weeks to gather the sheep for shearing, we left the balance of our stores in a small cupboard.

When the time came for us to return, some five weeks later, Alfie and I went on ahead of the others, the idea being that as the Rous Creek North Camp was long and narrow, we could manage to gather up the sheep on our own. The rest of the gang was to join us the following morning and together we would drive the flock of some 2,000 sheep back to the settlement for shearing.

It was a relief to see that the shanty was still there. For the first time, we were not faced with the task of having to erect the tent; come rain or shine, we would be able to eat and sleep in the dry. When we walked in through the door, it became clear that all was not well. The skins that we had left hanging on the wires were in shreds, stripped of every vestige of skin, all that was left were a few strands of wool.

The reason was obvious, Mice were everywhere, dozens of them. In the cupboard, under the blankets, nesting in small piles of wool and paper, clearly the labels from the canned food in the cupboard. There was not a crumb to be seen. We had left four packets of crispbread biscuits standing one on top of the other in the cupboard. The waxed packets were still there but a small tell-tale hole in the bottom of the lowest one led on up to the next and the next, every crumb of the contents was gone. It did not matter what we picked up, the mice had been there before us, and were still there.

The reason for the invasion and method of entry was equally clear. Where we had been unable to put the skirting around the floor, a gap had been left between the wall and the floor. Hence for the mice, an open door, and what's more a banquet of sheep skin and biscuits. We went hungry that night, with the exception of the cold meat that we had brought with us. Sleep, too, was difficult. The feeling that we were not alone under the blankets was never far away.

ROUS   CREEK

CHAPTER 11

EGGS FOR BREAKFAST

The 1914 battle of the Falklands was commemorated on December 8th each year by a public holiday, leading to a long weekend. Alfie, Peter and I talked over a few things that we wanted to do during the weekend. It was a beautiful evening with not a breath of wind and clear blue skies, the water in the harbour as calm as a mill pond. Tommy Skilling had gone out to Shallow Harbour for the weekend, leaving the three of us to amuse ourselves, without getting into too much trouble, or if we did, hopefully no one would get to hear about it. Alfie offered the thought that we should get up at first light, take the station dinghy and outboard motor and go to Fox Island, right at the mouth of the Philomel Pass and almost out into the open sea, to collect gull eggs to add an element of variety to our diet and excitement into our day. The need to start out at first light was very important, as by eight or nine o'clock in the morning the wind would freshen, not only increasing the risk to our safety, but adding to the effort required to keep away from the centre of the tidal path which would then be running strongly out of the harbour. The waters around the islands were no place to be in an open boat at any time of the year, and Fox Island, situated as it was close to the open sea, was among the last places to go for an outing.

The dinghy and outboard motor had not been used for some weeks and, with the tide rising, there was no time like the present to get them both in the water, check that the boat was seaworthy and the motor in good, efficient, working order, the next day's trip would take about half an hour each way with just a twenty minute rest, while the eggs were collected.

We worked with fervent enthusiasm and soon had the boat in the water and the outboard motor secured to the stern, Peter jumped into the dinghy, while Alfie and I offered advice and encouragement from the jetty. After a few sharp pulls on the starter-cord, the two stroke engine burst into life, hesitantly at first and then moved into full power. Peter suddenly found for himself a new sense of freedom. He was in his element as he circled around the inner harbour a few times and then at full throttle aimed the boat at the rocks on the shore. With inches to spare, he threw his entire weight to one side of the boat, at the same time pushing the rudder in the opposite direction, causing the boat to stand on its stern, do a 180 degree turn and head back out into the harbour, a game which only came to an end after a few near misses. Peter looked for a new game to play and soon found one, taking the little boat in under the jetty and out the other side at full throttle. For Peter, this was living life to the full. Alfie was not so sure. He had the responsibility of ensuring that all the farm boats were well maintained and cared for and he was almost beside himself with fear that Peter was about to wreck the boat.

No amount of pleading or suggested alternative methods to satisfy his craving, distracted Peter from his new-found fun, round and round he went, under one side of the jetty and out the other, stopping only to fill the engine with more fuel and check over the controls.

There was, however a vital check that he had neglected to make. As he continued his circling of the harbour with the throttle of the motor fully open, the tide was still rising and the gap between the water and underside of the jetty decreasing. Where half an hour earlier he had been able to stand up in the boat as it sped under the jetty, it was now necessary for him to crouch low to avoid striking his head and being tipped overboard.

Then it happened. The continuous jerking of the throttle, which formed part of the rudder control, caused the motor to shake loose from the stern of the boat and, suddenly, with a flurry of bubbles and a cascade of steam, it broke free, sinking to the bottom of the harbour in about ten feet of water. There was a few seconds' silence as we looked at each other and considered the situation in disbelief. A sobering influence overtook us as we realised that recovery was highly unlikely while the tide continued to rise and it would probably have to rest on the sandy bottom until the morning. Hopes for our run out to Fox Island seemed to disappear as quickly as the boat's motor.

From the dinghy's now-stationary position, we tried to hook onto the motor with grappling irons for some time, hoping to raise it to the surface before the penetrating saltwater started its corrosive destruction, but it was hopeless. The failing light forced us to give up the quest and the motor had to remain where it had come to rest until low tide some hours later would enable us to recover it with comparative ease.

With hopes dashed, three crestfallen and apprehensive crew went back to the cookhouse, to await the dawn of a new day and a somewhat uncertain future. Neither prizes or medals were offered for losing such a valuable piece of equipment as the station's only outboard motor. The only reason for us not getting the sack for a misdemeanour of such magnitude was attributable to the fact that the shearing season was just getting underway and it would be difficult to recruit a replacement gang. Three a.m. came quickly. It was a bright and wide awake Alfie who, refreshed from a few hours rest and, with renewed confidence, announced, not at all quietly, that we would row to Fox Island. Despite the early hour, the response was swift and positive, two voices with one accord quickly conveyed the unambiguous message. No way! Three o'clock in the morning was one thing. Three o'clock and the prospect of rowing a boat for three hours was something else, as without the motor on the boat the time for the journey would be doubled. Peter was prepared only to help Alfie down with the boat and recover the outboard motor before returning to his bed.

Alfie then set out undeterred, with Nick, his constant four legged companion at his heels, willing, largely through ignorance, to follow his master. It was some five hours later when a jubilant Alfie came bounding up the stairs armed with the cook's largest frying pan full of sizzling gull eggs. For the next week and beyond we were to have eggs with everything, boiled, fried, poached and scrambled, breakfast, lunch and supper, and with plenty left to take up the track to Bill Paice.

Alfie confessed to us later that the journey had not been without incident. Gulls in their hundreds, angry at their nesting ground being invaded and with a natural instinct to protect their eggs, had launched a violent and noisy attack which sent Alfie diving for cover in the rocky crevices of the shoreline and Nick, tail between his legs, cowering in the bow of the dinghy. Alfie's return roused Peter and I from our beds, more out of the need to strip down the outboard motor as quickly as possible than anything else. It could have been reasonably expected that the saltwater would have penetrated the engine and carburettor, but perhaps more in hope than expectation, it was also possible that a wash with fresh water, followed by a period submerged in a light oil would enable it to be used once again. We took it into the carpenter's shop where Alfie secured a thick board between the end of his work-bench and the tool locker, with the intention of clamping the outboard to it in a manner similar to that which it had been on the stern of the boat. Once secured Peter wiped it dry as best he could, changed the spark plug and decided to give the starter one defiant pull, more in anticipation that it would disgorge some of its salt water than in expectation that it would start. But burst into life it did, which with hindsight was equally as unfortunate as losing it in the first place.

Starting as it did, without adequate support and stability, caused it to wrench free from its temporary wooden support, belching blue smoke and spraying salt water in all directions. As it fell, the propeller, small as it was but revolving furiously, struck the side of the bench, causing the machine to catapult across the carpenter's shop, where it not only struck another piece of rigid structure but then careered back across the wooden building.

It was at that point that Peter and I decided that the carpenter's shop, twenty feet long and ten feet wide as it was, was still insufficient to contain three men, one of whom had never made a practice of being out in front when the call was made to perform brave acts. We rushed out leaving Alfie to tame the flailing beast, which fortunately did not prove too difficult. The motor, having exhausted itself of the petrol left in the carburettor, coughed, just once and stopped.

Saltwater having finally penetrated its precision parts. We hid the motor well out of sight in the carpenter's shop hoping beyond hope that Bill Paice would not come up with a reason to use it before we were able to give it a complete overhaul.

In starting as it did, the rogue machine dried out most of the water, but left many hours of work in stripping it down and reassembling, before it was eventually able to be used as it had been intended. Fortunately Bill made no call on its services, although he became aware of the extensive cleaning that it underwent. He did ask one or two searching questions, which suggested that there was a nagging doubt in his mind about the honesty and sincerity of his team who, when the chips were down, were rather inclined to close ranks in order to protect one another.

Alfie had undertaken to paint the provision store for the princely sum of £25 with the farm providing the paint. The colour scheme, in keeping with tradition, was white walls with green for the roof, double doors and windows. There was one handicap, he had promised Bill that he would get most of it done over the holiday weekend, weather permitting, which without doubt it was and he was keen to get started. We had all had our fill of gull eggs, the yolks were earmarked for scrambled egg to be eaten during the weekend, while Peter was converting the whites into meringues of all description, round ones, flat ones, risen ones, burnt and undercooked ones, with still two gallons of frothy mixture to spare.

Alfie was flushed with success, pride and a liberal glass or two of Booths gin. He had already put in the equivalent of a full day's work, but a promise was a promise and come what may, was going to be honoured. So with a carefree attitude he set about collecting together his paint and brushes. Peter, meanwhile, was looking for ways to put his surplus whipped egg whites to good use. One way was to flick a cupped handful at Alfie as he attempted to open the five litre can of green paint. In full spirit, or was it full of spirits, he joined in Peter's game until they became so wound up that Alfie called a halt. He had to get on with the painting, if only the lid would come off, which was more than reasonably secure. With a childish screech of laughter befitting any forty-year-old, he called Peter to come and give him a hand, which was little short of fatal. Peter's reputation for never knowing when to stop was running true to form, and was still a long way from being reached. Without hesitation, and before any attempt could be made to stop him, he lifted up a lump of concrete weighing at least three pounds above his head and brought it crashing down on the lid of the can of paint.

The can opened alright, albeit not in the prescribed manner. A wall of olive green gloss paint, of excellent quality and a well known brand, drifted up and then across a very large area of freshly painted, but dry, white wall, splattering over two windows as it went.

Such an act had a sobering effect on not only the offenders but also on those called on to help clear up, which was not an easy task. We tried to clean the paint off with a turps substitute that had the unfortunate effect of blistering the newly-painted white underneath. Paraffin was the agent most suited for separating the green from the white, but even that left the hitherto shining surface dull and lifeless, a marked hint of pastel green remained to contrast against the area of white that had escaped the deluge. There was no time to repaint the store before Bill Paice came down to inspect Alfie's handy-work.

An excuse had to be found and one that would stand up to a certain amount of questioning. The excuse was right there and, more than plausible, bright eyed, with a wagging tail, Nick the dog.

The well-rehearsed story described how Nick had bounded up to his master who, unfortunately, was carrying a large and opened tin of paint, with the result that the tin was knocked from Alfie's grasp and the paint distributed, for all to see, over a large area of the store! Alfie did get paid for his outstanding effort, it just took a little longer than originally estimated.

CHAPTER 12

FROM SIX UNTIL LATE

It was difficult to comprehend that Christmas fell in the height of summer, altering the context in which we had been brought up to expect the festive season.

Church services in the camp were non-existent. Fresh fruit and traditional Christmas fare were conspicuous by their absence. Turkey was definitely not on the menu and because of the protection afforded to it, neither was lamb. Sheep were bred solely for the production of wool. To kill a lamb meant that no wool would be produced from that animal, a £50 fine made sure that every lamb which finished up in the oven arrived there disguised as mutton. In spite of that, the odd mistake did occur. A more likely substitute, to take centre place at the Christmas lunch table was a piece of pork, particularly if someone in the settlement, keen to vary his diet, raised a pig but even that was likely to be a rare treat. The commercially operated butchery in Stanley was unlikely to have pork as a regular feature on the counter. For those living in the camp a wild goose or a piece of beef would probably be the main dish to grace the table on Christmas Day.

Picnics and leisurely time-consuming rides out into the camp were favoured pastimes for holiday recreation. The penguin rookery, with the young already hatched, was a popular place to visit, either to take yet more photographs - for the visitor and the resident alike photography attracted keen interest - or simply to sit and watch the comic antics of the adult penguins as they made an elaborate display of everything they did, particularly when another adult, having temporarily lost the location of its own nest, ventured too close.

For the single men living in the cookhouse, without close family association nearby, and limited places to visit, Christmas could be seen as no more than a welcome day off from the seemingly-endless round of shearing and dipping, although the families within the settlement made the single men welcome at all times. With the memory of past Christmas celebrations at home, there was usually an element of hope that it would soon be behind us. The hospitality, always warm and well intended, made it inevitable that loneliness and the feeling of isolation would creep in, particularly during family-centred occasions. In some instances, it was truly a relief to get back to work where we were, to a large extent, equal.

A typical day during the shearing season started just before six o'clock, sufficient time to get up and have a mug of black steaming hot coffee. The origin or reason unknown, it was common practice for the first coffee of the day to be that left over from the night before. The cook having started his day at three o'clock made it one of his first tasks to re-heat the coffee to near boiling point.

Turn-to time was six o'clock, not ten seconds after. The requirement was that the gang should be in the shearing shed, ready to catch their first sheep on the dot of the appointed hour. The shed was of sufficient size to hold a thousand sheep and divided into a series of pens, which decreased in size towards the front.

The front pens, outside of which the shearer worked, held about ten sheep. It was from those pens that the sheep were caught, sat down so that their feet were off the ground and carried, or slid, to the shearing floor to be clipped. Then, using hand shears and with the sheep still held in a sitting position, the belly wool was removed first and then the inside of the rear legs. The position was then changed and shearing continued up the neck and around the head, down the left-hand side and around the tail, changing position again to pick up the sheep at the head and shear down the right-hand side to finish at the rump. As each shorn sheep was let outside through a sliding door, a wool boy quickly gathered up the fleece, lifting it first by the neck and then gathering up the remainder in his arms. He took it to a large slatted table where, still holding the neck, he would throw it out across the table where an experienced grader stripped off the fine neck wool and the coarse pieces around the legs, throwing them into separate bins. The sides of the fleece were then folded into the centre and rolled, as tightly as possible, from the tail towards the neck, which was then twisted and stretched to form a band which was wrapped around the fleece to hold it together. Finally, depending upon its quality, it was thrown into one of the three large bins to await being pressed into bales. The fleece of a fully grown sheep weighed between five and seven pounds.

Breakfast was at eight o'clock, a forty minute break in which to eat four or six roast chops, gravy and two pieces of thickly sliced bread. "Smoko", was a ten minute break morning and afternoon, when the cook was required to bring tea to the shearing shed. An hour for lunch totalled our only respite during the eleven and a half hour day, often followed by a compulsory two hours' overtime, pressing the wool into five hundredweight bales.

The press was a seven feet high, open ended wooden box, with walls three inches thick and hinged on all corners. When filled with carefully positioned fleeces the box was pushed under a fixed steel block, the bottom similarly of steel was supported in the middle by an eight or ten inch diameter steel ram. Once positioned the ram was pumped up by hand to compress the seventy or so fleeces into a bale about one half of their original size. The pressed bale was then secured by steel bands and stitched into a hessian cover, before final branding with the station mark ready for shipment to the United Kingdom wool sales.

Shearing a sheep for the first time was quite frightening - not only for the sheep. We were constantly aware that the razor- sharp, pointed shears could inflict a fatal wound to the unfortunate animal. The tendency was for the inexperienced shearer to try to lift the wool from the back or side and in so doing lift the skin as well, which resulted in numerous small cuts and nicks which unless treated, presented a risk of infection.

To shear a sheep with the scissor-like hand shears took the average shearer between three and five minutes. On my first attempt, Bill Paice would not allow me to start before breakfast, because he thought that the two hours available was insufficient to complete the task. As usual he was right! Having shorn one sheep, the job quickly became easier and I was soon able to join the ranks of an average shearer.

Rivalry to clip the highest daily total was keenly fought, encouraged by a bonus of twopence halfpenny for each sheep shorn. The most proficient shearers turning out between 100 and 150 sheep each day. It was not unusual to try to hamper the progress of a colleague with whom we were in competition. There was no finer way of doing so than by offering his sheep a few blades of grass, implying that the job was taking so long that he, the sheep, must surely be getting hungry.

After pressing the wool into the near square bales, they had to be rolled down the jetty. In places where the jetty was particularly long, it was not unusual to find a track, on which ran a trolley, fitted with bogie wheels similar to those found on railways. Out of necessity the trolley was particularly heavy having to sustain the weight of a bale.

After extending and re-decking the jetty at Fox Bay, a team set about the task of building a trolley and installing suitable tracks from the shearing shed down to the end of the jetty. Sleepers had to be secured with four eighteen inch long bolts, each one drilled by hand with a wood auger. At the end of the track a wooden buffer was built to prevent the trolley crashing into the side of the boat which would be waiting to take on board the bales of wool.

Some weeks were spent preparing and laying the track, making sure that it was level, with the exception of the initial slope at the shearing shed, where the incline was sufficient to carry the trolley, without effort, to the end of the jetty. With a boat due within a few hours the gang hurriedly made the last section of the track secure. A major improvement to the farm's resources such as an extended jetty called for something of an official opening. Six of the station's fittest men, all of whom had been engaged in the lengthy job of building the track, were hastily assembled and seated on the trolley and given a hearty push to claim the dubious distinction of being the first to travel the new jetty on wheels. The trolley moved freely, a vindication of all the speculation that it was too heavy or that the track was out of alignment.

With the jetty being comparatively short, the journey had hardly started when the realisation came that the trolley was not going to stop without a serious collision with the buffer. Not wishing to be catapulted over the top and into the sea, the passengers leapt off either side, leaving the trolley to travel on alone, which it did with devastating results. The buffer, in spite of being constructed from two heavy sleepers standing on edge and bolted together, splintered into a dozen pieces, derailing the trolley as it did so. It overturned not once but twice, ending up disappearing from sight over the end of the jetty and into about fifteen feet of water - the labour-saving scheme coming to an end before it started.

Once again they seemed to be confronted with the impossible. The trolley, weighing about one ton presented two problems. The first proved to be comparatively easy, that involved locating the lost vehicle with the aid of grappling irons, then securing a stout rope around the axle. The second task called for ingenuity and resourcefulness, both essential requirements for survival every day. On this occasion only patience was required, just until the boat that we were expecting came alongside and was able, without any effort at all, to winch the trolley clear of the water and back onto the rails. It was a simple job to carry on with transporting the bales of wool to the stop at the end of the tracks, now little more than firewood. The only difference from the first journey was that the trolley was much slower and controlled.

CHAPTER 13

DRAMA ON GUN HILL

Rounding up sheep was not always without its excitement and drama. Gathering Gun Hill camp from the Chartres Point back to the Narrows was a distance of some eight to ten miles long and about four miles wide. There were four of us on one particular occasion: Alfie, Peter, young George and myself. Bill Paice was unwell and had stayed at home, trusting George to do his best. He could manage both dogs and horses well, but he hated having to get the peat in for his mother, so when the opportunity presented itself, for him to get away for a few hours with his dog, he responded eagerly.

We were to gather the ewes prior to dipping and our plan was to ride as far as the Chartres Point, passing the shanty at Gun Hill on the way. Having reached the point, we would spread out to cover the width of the camp, then drive the sheep ahead of us back as far as the shanty where we were to spend the night, as once darkness fell the sheep would be reluctant to carry on. Providing that it was a dark night, they would lay down and wait for the morning light. Consequently for all practical purposes, it was in our interests to carry on until that point was reached. The tricky part was to be back before first light and the sheep had a chance to disperse. The next day we intended to drive them as far as the Narrows and, leaving them in paddocks in the valley, we would then go on into the settlement for the night, returning the next morning to take the complete flock of about 3,000 sheep into the settlement.

All went well the first night. The sheep hardly had moved when we returned shortly after five o'clock the next morning. Peter took up his position in the gather on the South side of the camp which was bordered by Port Philomel, George and I took the top of the wide ridge, while Alfie took the north side bordering Christmas Harbour. The worst part for him was Town Point, jutting out as it did into the harbour. Although fenced off to prevent the sheep getting into the sand dunes, there were a number of places where the fence was broken which allowed the sheep to get through. The sheep knew every weak spot in the fence and, regardless of the occasion, would head for those places, when disturbed in order to escape. One well known "weak link" was in the fence that divided the respective camps of Fox Bay East and Fox Bay West. One sheep, very much an individual, was known to have avoided the shearer and the dip for three or four years by heading for one particular break in the fence. When eventually caught, sheep such as this one were invariably killed on the spot, skinned and the carcass left for the scavengers, as were sheep that were unable to keep up with the rest of the flock during a gather.

Our gather went well until about mid-morning. It was a fine, dry day and, although the wind was very strong, it was in our favour, encouraging the sheep to run on ahead. I became aware that I had not seen Peter for some time.

His area of gather was quite difficult, not particularly in terms of distance that he had to travel, but running very steeply from the top of the ridge where George and I were, down to the coast-line of Port Philomel, thick with fachine bushes and a maze of sheep tracks running the length of the ridge at different levels, very much like the contours on a map, but far too steep for tracks to run vertical to the shore-line, so steep in fact that when on horse-back following a sheep track, the rider's shoulder was only about two feet from the side of the hill. It was necessary either to lead the horse or, if already on, stay on. From the sheep track that the rider was on, to the one immediately below, was an almost sheer drop. Gathering under those conditions was impossible without a dog to work for you and keep the sheep moving.

George was far away to my right. For me to have broken off from the gather to go and look for Peter, without George knowing, would have left the camp wide open for the sheep to turn back between us, or tuck themselves away behind some rocks and be left behind. All I could do was to keep moving forward and hope that Peter was simply out of sight below me. He was riding a young colt that had only recently been purchased, with others, from New Island. The colt was almost certainly nervous having to travel along a narrow track.

As time passed without any sign of Peter, I decided to go and look for him, I pushed the sheep that I had in front of me, as far ahead as I could, which gave me time to make my way down the side of the ridge on foot and back to where I thought that he might be. I found him bruised and a little battered, trapped by the leg under the colt, and in the process of trying to untangle himself, without causing the horse to take fright. The horse had slipped from the narrow ledge and slid down to the lower track a few feet below, in doing so, he had laid on the side of the hill refusing to move, effectively pinning Peter to the ground.

When I reached him, he was expressing feelings of anger and relief, mad with himself, mad with the horse and above all mad with the sheep that had made it necessary for him to be there in the first place. It was very rare that serious accidents became a feature of working with animals, surprisingly enough when the remoteness of homes, the rugged terrain and the amount of time spent by men, women and children with horses was considered.

While I was looking for Peter, Alfie was on the opposite side of the camp overlooking the sea having a drama of his own. A small cut of about six sheep broke away from his dog and ran straight down the side of the hill and towards Town Point. Nick, always prepared to disobey the rules applying to the conduct and good behaviour of sheep dogs, chasing them both further and faster, with Alfie, livid with rage at both the dog and the sheep, in hot pursuit. The only escape for the sheep, as they saw it, was to head straight into the sea.

It was not unknown for Nick to take hold of a sheep at any convenient point and hang on until either dislodged or he brought the sheep down. On this occasion, the sheep were intent on keeping a sizeable gap between themselves and the dog.

With the fully-grown sheep swimming out to sea, Alfie tried to persuade Nick to swim around them and drive them back to the shore. Co-operation was not the order of the day, possibly due to the fact that, still very angry, he was trying to control the dog with typical Anglo Saxon phrases, none of which were terms of endearment.

It was very important not to leave behind any sheep when gathering for shearing and for the prudent man who carried a pair of shears with him, it was quicker to catch the weaker sheep and shear them there and then, but when gathering for dipping it was vital to bring them all in. If that proved impossible, the animal had to be destroyed out in the camp. Although it appeared callous and unnecessarily destructive, many had to be destroyed to prevent the spread of parasites and cull out unprofitable grades of wool. This time Alfie was literally between the devil and the deep blue sea, determined not to be beaten, and to show who was Boss. He rode his horse out into the sea so that he could come alongside each of the swimming sheep in turn and, leaning over, dispatched each one with a swift stroke of his sheath knife.

Unknown to Alfie, his private venture was being watched by George who had ridden over to the north side of the ridge, and from his vantage point, half a mile away, he saw it all unfold, had he not, this story like many others, would have gone unrecorded.

We successfully penned the sheep in Isthmus Cove, below the Narrows and rode into the settlement, arriving there late in the afternoon. Bill was still unwell and sent word that he would see us before we set out again the next morning. Alfie was clearly short tempered when we left the settlement soon after breakfast the next morning. Bill Paice had, as promised, come down to the cookhouse and spoken at length to Alfie, supposedly about the sheep that we were going to collect.

The reason for his attitude, clearly the substance of their conversation, became clear a few minutes later when we met George, who was greeted with a curt good morning and offered the advice that should he observe any unconventional methods of sheep gathering that day, it would benefit mankind generally and Alfie in particular, if he would keep it to himself.

Dipping was the last major task of the season. The dip, either of wood or concrete construction, resembled a long trough about five feet deep and twenty five feet in length. At each end were a series of pens of varying sizes, not unlike those in the shearing shed, where the pens decreased in size as they got closer to the seat of the action and built with the intention of making it easier to catch the sheep without any unnecessary pulling and pushing. Older sheep, having had the unhappy experience of being plunged into the cold, foul-smelling water on a number of occasions, often had to be dragged every inch of the way before finally being pushed into the dip. The pens at the opposite end were used to contain the sheep while some of the dip drained from their wool. Thousands of gallons would have been wasted had the sheep been allowed to run free immediately they came out of the dip.

CHAPTER 14

WHO DARES WINS

Sports week, towards the end of February, was an occasion to look forward to with great excitement. Each of the seven sheep stations on the West Falklands would take it in turn to host the week-long annual sports. Visitors would descend on the chosen farm from all over the islands, by horse, Land Rover, boat and aeroplane. No form of transport was excluded it seemed to bring folk from far and wide to enjoy the week long high-jinks. Each came with their own particular interests, horse racing and foot events every day, steer riding, dancing from dusk until dawn.

Every house and spare corner was pressed into service to provide a sleeping place for the visitors, with food, much of it cooked and prepared in the week before the holiday, always available. Set meals were impossible, the sheer volume of people and the marked absence of space saw to that. Music for the dances, held in a hastily-converted shearing shed, was provided by many willing musicians playing fiddle, violin and accordion, with Scottish tunes being thumped out hour after hour. Two full nights of Highland Schottische and the Gay Gordons were needed before the dust settled sufficiently to see clearly across the dance floor.

This only served to provide an excuse, if ever one was needed, for plenty of liquid refreshment. A goodly number of fractured limbs, from falls during the daytime activities, took a week to manifest themselves, such was the anaesthetised state of many of the participants.

These were the times when the barriers of absence of other people fell away and the pressure of solitude were reversed into a concentrated and semi-controlled barrage of dance and competition.

Of the sports, horse racing, steer riding and foot events were the three principal attractions around which each day's activities were centred. A flat piece of camp, within walking distance of the settlement, was roped off and designated the racecourse. The horses selected to race were the swiftest and most agile of the working horses. Rarely, if ever, was a horse kept solely for racing, although it was usual for the keen competitor to purchase a horse for its racing potential as well as its ability to do a day's work.

The foot sports, in which all could take part, ranged from the wheelbarrow race to the pillow fight on the greasy pole, and running events covered the 100 yard sprint to the measured mile, the latter guaranteed to test the stamina of the competitor suffering from over-indulgence the previous evening.

Steer riding drew the biggest gathering of spectators and rarely did a shortage of participants fail to meet the spectators' desire for thrills and spills. The image created by the cowboy film star of the ferociousness of the bucking steer at the Wild West Rodeo, was comparable to the steer-riding competitions which dominated a day in sports week.

The gauntlet, once thrown and accepted, was to find the bravest and surest rider. The young and fit would risk almost certain injury rather than retract the challenge. The objective of the ride was two-fold, first to stay on longer than anyone else and, secondly, to ride the steer to total submission so that he could slide off, perhaps exhausted by the ordeal, but as conqueror.

The steer was pushed and pulled into a narrow pen-like cage, wide enough only for the rider to ease himself to a position almost over the shoulders, then with one hand take a firm, vice-like grip on the rawhide strap, secured behind the front legs and over the back which, in turn, was secured to a second length of rawhide that ran under the tail or around the flanks. As the steer twisted, the rider tightened his grip to support himself, which tightened the kicking strap and encouraged the animal to buck, twist and turn even more.

"Who dares wins", as a challenge, barely entered the competition as the writhing, leaping, bellowing beast was released into the crudely roped enclosure, as it tried to free itself of the encumbrance on its back.

With his free hand held high, thrashing the air as if seeking support and balance, the rider attempted to keep his eyes firmly fixed on the ears of his unwilling mount, in so doing he ensured that his own body twisted and turned in the same direction. The two would soon part company and another rider bite the dust, only to stagger off into the crowd and join in cheering the next challenger who dared to tempt both fate and providence.

The end of the week came all too quickly and Saturday brought with it a return to isolated homes and solitude, with the sound of accordian music ringing in our ears as a reminder of the week now passed, if ever a reminder was needed.

CHAPTER 15

PETER'S BLACK LOOK

With the population of the camp being predominantly male, it was inevitable that the occasional skirmish would occur. Nevertheless, fighting in any form was actively opposed and frequently led to the sack for the aggressor, always assuming that drink had not played a part in the affray. In cases where drink had featured neither the Farm Manager or the Foreman would take sides in apportioning blame.

One evening, Peter and Alfie came to blows. What had started out as rough horseplay finished up with fists and furniture flying in all directions in an all-out fight. I was upstairs in my room reading when the crash and bang of disintegrating furniture signalled that things were getting out of hand. I went downstairs to find the oil lamp swinging wildly on its hook in the wooden ceiling above the dining table. Tommy Skilling was sitting in his usual place by the galley door, elbows resting on the table, puffing on his pipe, quite unmoved by the carnage that was being enacted on the floor before him. His verbal utterances alternating between questions like, "Why are you fighting you daft gentlemen? Someone is going to get hurt in a minute". To words of encouragement like, "Hit him again before he gets up and kills ya". The battle went on for some minutes with Alfie, the older of the two, emerging the worse for wear, sporting what was clearly going to develop into two black eyes, a bloody nose and a jagged piece removed from his left ear, which was bleeding profusely. The furniture too had suffered badly in the affray, with one armchair reduced to standing on three legs, curtains torn down from the window and a small stool damaged beyond repair, having at some stage in the proceedings been used as a weapon, which had fortunately missed its intended victim and cannoned into the chimney breast and neatly divided it in two. Alfie, not being an aggressive person, was clearly upset by both the skirmish and the outcome. After a few minutes weighing up the situation and wanting to get his side of the story told first, he set off up the track to acquaint Bill Paice with the fact and to prevail upon his wife Annie's good nature and first aid box to dress his injuries. Having got from Alfie an assurance that neither he or Peter had been drinking, Bill promised to remonstrate with Peter at the earliest opportunity after tempers had been allowed to cool, a fact that Alfie was only too pleased to acquaint Peter with when he returned to the cookhouse some time later, suitably decorated with a bandage around his wrist and hand and a plaster on his ear.

The atmosphere had a distinct edge on it the next morning. Peter repeatedly looked up the track towards Bill's house to see if he was coming, becoming more and more agitated as the morning progressed. His attitude was very much like my own when trouble was expected, taking the view that it was better to meet the problem head-on, as it was unlikely to go away. At about eleven o'clock the figure of the Foreman was seen to emerge over the hill and towards the cookhouse.

The suspense proved too much for Peter. He went outside, climbed on his bicycle, which travelled with him from job to job, and rode off to meet his fate. With his usual air of defiance and bravado he rode a tight circle around the Foreman, too tight in fact, for in doing so he became parted from his bicycle and fell noisily and quite undignified at his feet. This latest display was seen as the final chapter in a long line of unacceptable events, which prompted the rather sharp and crisp question "What the hell do you think you are up to?" referring to the events of the previous evening. Quite unmoved and very much wrapped up in his bicycle, Peter replied, "I'm trying to get up and will do, when I can get my bloody foot out of these spokes", which was not the reply that Bill had been looking for. Once again Peter was asked to leave and accepted a month's notice, agreeing to leave on the next boat that called.

Peter was financially embarrassed at the time and asked Bill if he could put a coat of tar on the roof of the shearing shed before he left so that he would, at least, have enough money to pay for the boat fare into Stanley. Bill agreed, but warned him that although the weather was quite mild, winter was just around the corner and as a consequence it was plenty cold enough to try putting a thin coat of tar on a thirty foot high roof. Peter said that he would work weekends to get the job done, hoping that the weather would not become too changeable. In any event, once the sun had gone down in mid-afternoon, it would become too cold to work outside without gloves and protective clothing.

Bill, Alfie and I had another job to do. Bill's house, well away from the rest of the settlement and tucked away under a ridge that ran almost the entire length of the camp from the Narrows to Shallow Harbour, was having difficulty in getting sufficient fresh water to suit the needs of his household, so we set about damming off a small stream about three hundred feet above and behind the house. It was not the easiest of jobs standing in cold running water trying to create a barrier that would form the front of the dam. More than once it crossed my mind that Peter had the best job after all, even if he did have to work on his own. He was able to go into the cookhouse occasionally, to get warm. There was no fear that Tom would go out to see him, it was not necessary anyway, Tom could watch him from the galley window and store up points for criticism at some later date without going out into the cold.

Our job on the ridge was made more difficult by the odd snow flurry whipped up in the strong, biting wind. At about three o'clock in the afternoon Bill suggested we call it a day. We had been able to get the pipe required to convey the water to the house firmly embedded in the dam, the remaining task of getting air out of the pipe could wait until the next day. We had taken the tractor with us so it didn't take Alfie and I long to get back down to the cookhouse. Putting the tractor away, I decided, would have to wait until I had thawed out, hardly waiting for the tractor to stop, I jumped off and sprinted into the mess. Peter was already in and, although it was starting to get dark, Tom had not yet lit the oil lamp, but it was quite clear that all was not well. Peter's face looked strangely red, almost inflamed, he was quick to point out that it was burning as well, even before we had time to enquire the reason for his sudden and ruddy complexion.

There were many instances when our attitude towards our colleague's misfortunes seemed harsh and sometimes downright cruel but this time it was different. Peter was clearly in great discomfort and we had to find out why, or better still, what had happened to cause him to turn from a Pale Face into a Red Indian in such a short space of time. Tom took up the story and told us how he had been watching Peter out of the window as he brushed on the tar, which was clearly cold and stiff, making it difficult to spread. Peter had come down off the roof, filled up his tar pot and brought it into the galley to warm it up on the cooking stove in the galley. That had the desired effect of making the tar easier to spread. Wishing to get on with the job he went back over to the shed and climbed up the ladder. He had reached the top before realising that his brush was resting on a rock back down on the ground, wedging his tar pot between the slope of the roof and the top of the ladder he went back down, picked up the brush and made his way back up to the roof. He had clearly overlooked the fact that the ladder, being particularly long, bowed in the middle with his weight, which caused the few inches that protruded over the eaves of the roof to be reduced still further and as a result the pot of warm tar slipped from its precarious position, depositing the entire contents of the pot over his head.

They had been unable to summon help so under Peter's direction they had set about cleaning him up, using paraffin and methylated spirits which caused his ruddy complexion and obvious discomfort. Had they given it a few moments thought they would have realised that the pounds and pounds of sheep dripping in the larder, used for cooking, would have done the job with far less anguish and discomfort.

The solution was not so easy, something had to be done, but what? Once again the advice of Annie Paice was needed. Perching Peter on the drawbar of the tractor, I headed back up the track, leaving Alfie and Tom in the cookhouse. Annie decided that the doctor needed to be consulted without delay.

The choice was limited to trying the radio transmitter in the hope that someone would hear the call and be able to get a message to the doctor in Fox Bay. The only other option was to send a rider to the Chartres settlement, or to East Bay House, in the hope that the land line to Fox Bay was intact. In any event, either destination would have taken some hours riding time, after suitable horses had been caught and geared up.

Surprisingly for a Saturday afternoon, the call was picked up in Chartres and a telephone call quickly brought the doctor to the radio. With the assurance that the burning sensation was something that, in itself, was not serious and could be relieved by painting the patient's face with a weak solution of bicarbonate of soda and water, and the doctor's assurance that no permanent damage was likely to have been caused, we applied the cure. Fortunately the doctor was right. By morning, Peter was feeling better and we were able to enjoy a laugh at his expense for the next week. What we had not realised at the time was that the bicarbonate solution dried a brilliant white, so Peter had to walk around with two very red eyes and a mouth looking out through an expressionless white mask.

CHAPTER 16

THE HURRIED DEPARTURE

The hobby that captivated the interest of many people, in a situation cater-
ing for every taste from still life to landscape, marine life to wild birds,
was photography. Many of the Stanley stores appointed agents in the larger
settlements to sell their photographic equipment, with the choice available
suiting both the novice and professional. The more dedicated enthusiasts
developed, printed and enlarged their own films in improvised darkrooms.
Countless photographs and slides of sights and scenes were taken for no
other reason than to try to improve upon the last.

It was not unusual for inhabitants to take a "round trip" on one of the
passenger-carrying boats whose itinerary included calling at a number of
farms before returning to Stanley. Although only stopping for an hour or
two at each place, there was usually sufficient time to go ashore, meet
friends and take photographs.

Peter had always devoted much of his leisure time and money to
photography, a hobby that had led him, and me, into the unknown on a
number of occasions. However he remained disappointed that, in spite of
the countless number of photographs that he had taken over the years, there
were very few showing the marine life that we knew existed close to the
settlement. So it was, with the time of his departure drawing near, that he
asked me to go with him to Bullock Island, which was in the centre of
Philomel Pass, about fifteen minutes boat journey from the settlement, to

take some photographs of seals, sea-lion and elephant seals that we knew were there, living in the tussock grass.

Although it was cold, there was little wind as we set out shortly after lunch in the station dinghy, having first selected two pairs of oars from the Carpenters shop where they had been stored in the rafters for some months. Two pairs would enable us both to row and, therefore, help us through the incoming tide which we would be unable to avoid, in either our outward or return journey, as with darkness falling at about 3.30, there was no time to wait for the tide to turn. At Bullock Island we pulled the boat well up on to the rocks above the high water mark and climbed the short but steep sides of the island into the tussock grass, hoping that we did not come face to face with a seal or sea-lion before we had time to get our bearings and to get an idea of the shape of the island, which we knew to cover an area of about two acres. It had looked easy when viewed from the settlement, but once ashore took on an entirely different appearance.

The long succulent tussock grass grew in large clumps in the sandy soil, but erosion by the wind and rain, seal and sea-lion and the bullock which had been allowed to roam as they pleased for many years, largely undisturbed, now meant that the roots of the tussock were at shoulder height. The result was that we found ourselves walking through deep and narrow pathways which were all overhung with the long grass. Bill had assured us, on a number of occasions, that no one had reported seeing any bullock on the island for some years but we would be very unfortunate or, dependent on your point of view, fortunate, if we did not see plenty of sea creatures.

In keeping with my style of being a gentleman and confirmed coward when faced with the possibility of meeting the unexpected, I let Peter go first. He was the one with the camera and I had no wish to place at risk the possibility of his becoming famous with his marine life works of art. We made our way through the maze as carefully and as quietly as we could, catching the occasional glimpse of sea-elephant as it lumbered off disturbed by what was in any event our clumsy approach.

We congratulated ourselves on the fact that the island tenants had all been able to turn around in the narrow pathways, and in so doing avoid a confrontation, the outcome of which would certainly have been a hasty retreat by yours truly and friend, with me taking the lead.

Luck stayed with us and we soon came to a small clearing, near the centre of the island. There, basking in the sunshine and protected from the wind, was a group of about fifteen elephant seals. Apart from much grunting and snorting, they were content to stay in the opening and be photographed in varying poses and positions. We spent about twenty minutes watching, with interest and fascination, the battle-scarred bull elephant-seal keeping his cows together, occasionally moving in on a young male that came in too close. The wind had been increasing all the time and a sudden squall of driving sleet was enough to remind us of the need to make our way back to the boat. An unfamiliar noise caused us to turn towards the direction of the sound, there, to our horror and disbelief, stood an old, but clearly agile, white bullock, fitting very well the description given to us by Bill Paice, of the leader of the small herd which had lived on the island. There was neither the time nor the need to question Bill's earlier assurance that the last animal had disappeared some time before, as this one moved towards us, head lowered to show the full magnificence of his horns that spanned a full two feet, with the neat pointed ends facing forward, at us!

His quickening pace was our cue to leave, hopefully at a speed that would increase the gap between us. We twisted and turned in the narrow paths between the tussock. The need to look behind was both futile and unnecessary. The noise was all the confirmation necessary to urge us on, hopefully arriving at the beach, before we became the subject of an assisted passage. I had experienced bellowing cattle, many times before, either because they were hungry or desired to be milked. However this time it was quite different. This one was clearly not hungry and it was most certainly not the milking kind, it simply preferred to be left alone with the seal and the sea-lions, all of whom were unaccustomed to seeing people. I was quite prepared to give them all the space they required. The consequence of slowing down distracted our minds completely from the possibility of meeting large lumps of marine life ahead of us.

Rounding a sharp corner and with no hope of stopping, there lay before us a sleeping sea-lion. Avoiding it was out of the question, "needs must when the devil drives". Before he had time to weigh up the situation, one step took me on to his back and a second to his head and without a backward glance, I was some feet ahead of him.

Fortunately, Peter, unhappy at finding himself strategically placed between me and the advancing bullock, had chosen that moment to take another route between the tussock and we arrived on the beach at the same time from slightly different paths, relieved to know that we could at least see where we were going and assured that the bullock would not follow us onto the rocky beach.

Crisis behind us, we took stock of the situation. The tide was still rising and increased cloud was bringing with it more wintery squalls. It was time to go back to the settlement while there was still plenty of daylight. The return journey was not going to be as easy with both the wind and tide against us. We got into the boat and pushed off from the shore, both of us rowing, me in the bow and Peter about mid-ships. In order to get clear of the beach, we had to put considerable weight onto the oars. Without warning, one of my two oars snapped with a resounding crack that sent me sprawling on my back into the bow of the boat. The tide instantly swung the boat into the tidal flow and away from the settlement. As I struggled to regain my place, Peter passed me one of his oars while he, with his remaining oar, started to scull out over the stern.

The forces of the wind and tide rapidly took us towards Round Point which, although part of the mainland, jutted out like a jagged finger into Port Philomel. Within seconds, it seemed that we had been carried half a mile further away from the settlement. As I fought to pull us through the tide and into calmer water a second oar broke, just as clean as the first. It was becoming apparent that the oars, having been stored in the carpenters shop, had dried out to such an extent that they would not give under the weight of water being displaced. With only two oars left from our original four, Peter took both and fought desperately to take us clear of the point, from which we could now clearly see emerging, a sharp jagged reef. Another sudden squall made it impossible to see where we were or where we were going, it was quite hopeless. We grabbed an oar each and tried to ward off the rocks which we were now in real danger of being thrown onto by the swell and boiling water.

I had resigned myself to being thrown out of the boat, to almost certain death, when suddenly, without warning, we were lifted up by a wave, which instead of smashing us to pieces took us clean over the top of the reef and into the calmer waters on the other side. An unbelievable transformation took place both within and around us. The boat was back under our control, the sea was again our friend, taking us where we wanted to go, where only a few moments before it was prepared to take us to our deaths.

There were lessons to be learnt. Perhaps the most important one was that although the oars had been kept dry in the Carpenters shop it was equally as important to keep them oiled, thereby ensuring that they would flex and give when pressure was placed upon them as we had to do that afternoon. We arrived back at the settlement physically none the worse for our adventure, but hopefully wiser. If ever a salutary lesson was needed, we received one later that evening when the local news reported that the sea had claimed the lives of two of our acquaintances that same afternoon in Fox Bay harbour. There could be little doubt, with the wind in the direction that it had been, that the squall which had nearly caused our downfall, a few minutes later, had contributed to the deaths of our colleagues.

Peter's eventual departure from Dunnose Head came very much by chance. The boat that we had been expecting failed to materialise, it was not unusual for a boat to change its intended route. Alternative plans were made for him to fly to Stanley, where he hoped to get a job on one of the boats, leaving us to put his heavy luggage and bicycle on the next boat that called, which appeared to be some months away.

However, a sudden change in the *Darwin's* itinerary brought her to Dunnose Head, enabling him to leave with all his worldly belongings and join his sister in Stanley, with whom he invariably stayed when between jobs.

The reason for the change in the busy schedule of the *Darwin* was due to the delivery of a long-awaited piece of equipment, no less than a new Perkins diesel tractor to replace the old Cletrac which had finally reached the end of her days.

Taking possession of a new tractor was not without its difficulties and tense moments. The shallow sandy harbour meant that all our cargo had to be ferried by scow between the boat, anchored well out in deep water, and the jetty. To bring the three ton tractor ashore required two scows to be lashed together, with stout timbers, sufficient to carry the weight of the tractor, secured amidships across the top of both scows. The tractor was then lifted clear of the boat by her crane and gently placed on the timbers, leaving the motorboat to tow the top-heavy load ashore or, more to the point, where it ran aground in the shallow water. It was then that the tractor was no longer the responsibility of the ship but mine. I was to drive down an improvised ramp and into three feet of water which proved to be the least of my problems. The real difficulty was that, once moving, the tractor had to be kept moving down the ramp but when the weight of the tractor started to come off the scows they would then begin to float and move from side to side while the tractor was still perched precariously on the improvised ramp. There was the added risk that one or both sides of the ramp would slip off the scow and drop the lot into the water, including yours truly. Luck was on my side once again and the tractor made a safe passage to the beach and on to dry land. From that day the Cletrac gave up its dry shed to a more powerful machine.

For Peter the journey was put to good use and resulted in him being offered a job on the *Darwin*, which was really more than he had dared hope for. His hope for work on the boats had been restricted to the possibility of working on the very small boats in and around Stanley.

It was not just change for change's sake that had prompted him to seek work afloat, but rather his determination to overcome seasickness, a condition that plagued him every time that he came within spitting distance of a boat, regardless of its size. It would not have been unkind to say that if Peter looked at salt water, Peter got sick.

His position on the *Darwin* was that of Able Seaman, a most inappropriate title, which called for him, under instruction, to take his turn at the wheel when making the monthly voyage to Montevideo. To describe the tempestuous seas of the South Atlantic as heaving, twisting seas, within Peter's hearing, would have been unkind in the extreme. Nevertheless, heaving they were and he never failed to take up his position on the Bridge without a bucket firmly wedged between his feet and, following a particularly storm-tossed voyage to Punta Areanas in Chile, he gave up his quest for liberation from the debilitating condition of seasickness.

The *Darwin* made about two trips each year to Punta Areanas, usually taking a cargo of live sheep and returning with horses, coal and timber for building and fencing. Good travelling conditions enabled the journey to be completed in thirty six hours, but it was rarely that easy. The sea between the Falklands and the Straits of Magellan took the full force of winds from around Cape Horn. There were occasions when the ship was unable to make any headway at all. Sheep carried on deck in anticipation of a calm passage were frequently swept overboard when the weather conditions deteriorated to such an extent that to venture out on deck was nothing short of suicide. Such were the seas that pounded the shores of the much-loved islands.

CHAPTER 17

THE MISSING SHEEP

As the weeks spread into months, I moved back to Fox Bay just after the start of a new season. With the change came the opportunity to work in Packe's Port Howard which consisted of a house, shearing shed and dip. Although there was only one house, it was large enough to accommodate the Fox Bay gang when they were required to help with the sheep work at that end of the farm. The land owned by the company in that part of the West Falklands was dominated by a high ridge bordered on one side by the coastline of the Falkland Sound.

Gathering sheep from the top of the Coast Ridge camp, was not without its problems. My first experience coincided with gale force winds gusting to eighty miles an hour. Under such conditions it was difficult to stay on a horse, once off, almost impossible to remount, making it necessary to lead the horse down off the ridge and find a sheltered position behind a rock formation before attempting to get back on, then start looking for the rest of the gang, who had carried on with the gather, unaware of the difficulty that I had been having.

The winds were reminiscent of the occasions in Dunnose Head when leaving the cookhouse during a gale. So strong were they that in order to make any headway it was necessary to lean forward into the wind, and frequently when rounding a corner fall flat on your face because an adjacent outbuilding had obstructed the free passage of wind, eliminating the need to lean forward but too late to take any corrective measure.

At the end of a two-week spell of shearing and dipping, which had included some 3.00 a.m. starts ahead of a gather, and 8.00 p.m. finishes to get the wool pressed, we set out to return to Fox Bay. It had taken us seven hours to ride up but the return journey was planned to take three days as we were to take with us a flock of some 800 maturing lambs, between twelve and sixteen weeks old.

The route took us through the Port Howard settlement of J.L. Waldron, another absentee landlord. Going that way meant that we had to pass through a narrow driveway bordered on each side by a row of sheds, in which men were working. Rumours circulating later suggested that not all the plump, well fed lambs that went up the drive emerged from the other end.

We spent the first night at the Shag Cove shepherd's house, the second at the Blue Mountain shanty. Soon after midday on the third day, we turned the flock free into the Home Flock camp at Black Hill corner, about an hour's ride from the Fox Bay settlement. At that point Ken Spicer, a fellow expatriate, was detailed off by Mike Murphy to ride down through the Stud Paddock, gather up a small flock of about fifteen sheep and take them on into the settlement where I was to join him and together we would kill them for mutton.

We arrived in the settlement shortly after one o'clock and waited for Ken to arrive. By mid afternoon I started to feel concerned about his failure to appear at what I thought to be a reasonable time after our own arrival. Waiting for a further half an hour, I set out to look for him but fortunately I did not get far. From a vantage point at the top of the green I could see a figure, leading a horse and following a small cut of sheep, walking down the shale cutting that led into the Doctor's Creek, just a short distance from the settlement.

I waited for him by the gate at the top of the green, as he came nearer it was clear to see why he was walking. His horse, Spirit, had no riding gear other than a bridle, reins and a lead rein, whereas when we had left him at the top end of the Stud Paddock he had a full set of riding gear.

The expression on his face told most of the story and it did not take him long to fill in the remaining pieces of the jigsaw. Shortly after we had parted, he had picked a sufficiently large cut of sheep to bring on into the settlement, too large in fact, and in order to help his dog divide them up, he had ridden his horse, at some speed, into the centre of them. The horse tripped, supposedly over a sheep that had failed to move out of the way fast enough, and Ken was removed, quite unceremoniously, from his elevated position on Spirit's back. His horse, in turn, took fright and, in Ken's words, was last seen heading towards the settlement at an undetermined speed showing all the signs that the riding gear had come loose, as it slipped beneath the mare's body and was in the process of being kicked to pieces. Horses could be guaranteed to oppose having any loose material flapping about beneath their person.

The two fortunate things about the entire incident, which Ken was hoping to put quickly behind him, was that firstly he was still able to bring the sheep into the settlement and secondly Spirit, having got over her panic of the moment, rid herself of the loose riding gear, and was waiting patiently at the gate that led into the Doctor's Creek.

Ken devoted many hours, often with the help of myself and others, looking for his riding gear, to no avail, which only served to demonstrate the vastness of the camp and the sometimes difficult ground cover. It could have come off as the horse jumped a deep, steep sided stream, and fallen in, obscured from view by the overhanging banks, or it could have come free as Spirit cantered through the two-foot high fachine bushes, never to be seen again.

To everyone's surprise, a few weeks later, Spirit had a foal, which was almost certainly the reason for her nervousness and tension which, incidentally, had left me sitting on my backside in the stone corral at Port Howard, shortly after three o'clock on a frosty morning a few days before.

I was rarely thrown from a horse but I had the misfortune to fall off many times. My next mishap never seemed to be very far away. I set out a few days later, on my own, to gather up a small flock of about eighty sheep which were in the Ram Paddock, just north of the settlement, and drive them out into the Coast Ridge, a straightforward task that could have been expected to take about two hours.

My horse that afternoon had the unusual name of Simon, perhaps because unlike most horses, he showed a marked tendency to be quite simple. He stood about fourteen hands high with feet that could be best described as being, the size of dinner plates, and heavy with it, as many potential riders, including myself, found to our cost when we failed to move out of his way fast enough. Simon's most aggravating characteristic was that he positively hated being on his own, with the result that his rider, in this particular instance me, had to urge him on every inch of the way and that, under any circumstances, was hard work. The only time that he was prepared to move with ease was when he came within sight of the settlement, on the return journey. Then, the rider, having dismounted to open the gate, had to be quick in getting back on, for as soon as Simon felt the weight of a foot being placed in the stirrup, he was gone which, because of his height, frequently left the hapless rider swinging out to one side as the horse cantered at great speed towards the next gate.

With much coaxing and kicking we came across a cut of sheep just inside the Ram Paddock, which was very fortunate. The paddock covered an area of about seventy five acres and I had not the slightest inclination to waste time and effort looking for a few sheep. The sheep ran on ahead of us, well down into the Sand Hills and in the directions of the corner gate, that led into the Coast Ridge. The fence in that area had recently been renewed so I was not concerned when the sheep went into a small valley and out of sight.

I rode up to the gate and dismounted, at the same time putting my old dog out around the sheep, to bring them slowly up to the gate which would enable me to count them as they ran through. The only thing predictable about sheep was that if one did something the rest would attempt to follow, regardless of whether there was ten or ten thousand; if one jumped over a stick or ran around a puddle, so would every one that followed behind. My satisfaction at seeing this little lot pass from one piece of camp to the other was shortlived, as horror of horrors, there was only about fifty. I could not believe my eyes. My mind raced back over the sequence of events since gathering them up in the Ram Paddock.

There was only one conclusion possible. I had missed almost half of them, somewhere back by the Ram Paddock gate, and compounded the mistake by not recognising the obvious difference between fifty and eighty sheep. There was no time to waste now, the sun was getting well down in the sky and I was destined to be in real trouble if I ran out of daylight.

There was no alternative other than to ride all the way back to look for a few, well more than a few, sheep. Every one of which I could have cheerfully treated in the same way as Alfie had treated some of his in the Town Point camp some months previous. The saving grace for the ones that I had to look for was that I had nowhere to hide the carcasses of that number of sheep.

I swung into the saddle, saying quite audibly, but to no one in particular. "Simon, we are going to have to get a move on this time". We did! There was just the faintest sound of a metallic 'chink' as Simon backed into a short length of wire, carelessly left by the fence erectors. In much quicker time than it takes to recount the tale, Simon's rear end went up, his head went down, and I went through between his ears. I was upset. I ran through all the adjectives in my vocabulary, and started using some of them for the second time. Had the rapid, one sided and not very well animated conversation, that I had been having with my horse been overheard the listener would have been obliged to agree that I was upset.

My anguish having subsided, I tried for a second time to remount, and set out to look for the missing sheep. I was satisfied that they were not in the Sand Hills camp, so I rode straight back to the Ram Paddock gate. Simon sensed the need to be on his best behaviour, spurred on by the fear that he might tread on some more wire, we travelled well and were soon back at the gate that we had left a good hour before. I left the usual track and travelled through the sand dunes, looking for the sheep with an air of both desperation and anxiety. Hope springs eternal and it only took a few minutes to find the subjects which had been the source of my trouble grazing peacefully, close to the spot where I had found the others. It was with marked relief when I eventually took them through the Coast Ridge camp gate, just as the sun sank from sight.

It was quite dark as I rode Simon through the lead that took us into the settlement. Ken met us at the stables, he was about to gear up another horse to come and look for me. I treated his concern with surprise. After all, as I explained to him, it had been a nice afternoon and I had just taken things easy, having been content to walk most of the way, behind the sheep. The rivalry between us was well known, and he would have taken great delight at the knowledge of my afternoon's chapter of events, which would have brought into question my ability to handle horse, dog or sheep. It would also help to mitigate much of the guilt and loss of face that Ken, quite wrongly, felt had fallen to him since his chapter of unfortunate mishaps in the Horse Paddock.

PARTING COMPANY

CHAPTER 18

THE LITTLE RED COW

A Friday in the middle of March was a busy day in Fox Bay. First of all, the station horses had to be rounded up and the mares used for breeding had to be separated out from the troop with their foals, some of which were nine months old and quite a handful to catch. In all, some thirty foals had to be caught so that we could mark them with the company's brand, a crossed triangle. The stallion foals had to be castrated. It was a cruel test for both men and horses. First they had to be thrown, their legs tied and then branded with red-hot irons. The risk of being kicked was ever present.

To most people the difference between a stallion and a mare was obvious but on this occasion Ken Spicer, seemingly in complete ignorance, ask the fateful question, "How do you tell a horse from a mare?". The silence that followed was deafening. Total disbelief that anyone who had been working with animals, even for just a year or so, as in Ken's case, could really fail to observe the difference, when viewing the rear end of a horse from two feet away, with its tail tied back. However, he had asked the question and he was going to get an answer. It came crisp and clear, with no preamble or wasted words, from a somewhat stunned Station Manager, Wick Clements, "Dammit man, lift up its tail and see if its hat's on straight". Not a difficult expression to interpret and perfectly adequate even for the most unworldly animal lover.

We finished with the horses shortly before lunch. Mr. Clements was setting out for Dunnose Head immediately after he had eaten so before he left he called Ken and I together to give us work for the remainder of the day. Addressing us both he said, "Take the mares back to the Paddock, after which you, Roger, go on into the Stud Paddock, bring in some wethers and kill about ten for mutton. Ken, I want you to take my revolver and put down a calf that you will find at the top of the Horse Paddock. The cow got over onto her back, fell into a ditch and drowned". An all too frequent occurrence, sometimes distressing, but rarely avoidable.

We set off after lunch encouraged by the thought of being able to have a good canter up through the Horse Paddock, which was about a mile and a half from one end to the other. For Ken the thought of having the Boss's revolver was a touch of the Wild West and an exciting opportunity.

The horses we were riding went well, as was usual when following other horses. As we cantered up through the shale cutting and into the open camp, Ken went on ahead to open the gate and direct the mares into their own paddock, the entrance to which was just off the vehicle track that linked Fox Bay East to Fox Bay West. I rode up just as Ken dismounted from his horse and closed the gate behind the mares.

With a tone of confidence and satisfaction, he called out to say that he had just seen the calf on the other side of the hill as he came round to open the gate for the mares. "We'll go and do that next and then all that's left is the mutton to round up".

We found the calf, as Ken had said, and got down from our horses. It was a lovely animal, a strong red bull calf. There was no sign of its mother but the calf could have wandered off from where she had fallen in the ditch. Ken said that this must be the one, in spite of our reservations, it looked so strong and healthy, but it still left very little room for sentiment.

Sometimes it was a dog or a favourite horse that had to be shot. There was always room for care and compassion but rarely sentiment. We spent a few minutes looking around, there were no signs of any other animals. I said to Ken that he might as well get on with it, there was no point in waiting about any longer.

A dull thud was followed almost simultaneously by a deep bellow that caused Ken and I to turn towards the crest of the hill, around which he had ridden just a few minutes before. The sight that met our eyes was an incredible one but the fact was indisputable. The angry and protective cow which was coming towards us, head down and bellowing, was clearly the mother of the calf that Ken had shot a split second earlier.

With a sudden realisation of the consequence of our actions I responded with a few sharp words. "Let's get the hell out of here". My horse was well aware of the source of danger. By the time my right leg had slid over the saddle, we were already at full canter up the track that went right to the top of the Horse Paddock. We rode without a backward glance for some minutes, my mind racing at an equal pace, drawing little satisfaction from the fact that the job of getting rid of the calf had clearly been given to Ken. As we drew together, Ken seemed to look to me for answers. He certainly had nothing to contribute to the obvious. My own observations were unrepeatable. It was unbelievable. Hadn't we checked, looked for other animals, done all that was required of us? Then the real questions. Where had the boss said the calf was? What colour had it been? How old did he say it was? And not least of all the questions. If that was the wrong one, where was the calf that we had been sent to look for?

Although we were travelling together, we had been given separate tasks to do and it seemed sensible that we help one another, but the truth of the matter was that I hadn't listened to the detail of Ken's instructions and he had allowed the prospects of having Mr. Clements' revolver strapped to his waist, distract him from the essential element of his mission. After much questioning and recall of the detailed instructions, it emerged that the subject of our mission had been black and white, about one week old and at the north end of the Horse Paddock. The one that Ken had shot had been red, about one month old, and at the extreme south end of the paddock.

Three things were at the forefront of our minds as we sought to consolidate our position. Whose calf had we shot? Its mother, in full milk, should have been in the settlement. What if someone came across the calf, a remote possibility, but it was close to the track and someone might travel that way. Mr. Clements would use that route on his return from Dunnose Head. But the nagging issue, that refused to go away was, where was the black and white calf? We searched high and low, criss-crossing backwards and forwards over an area of about fifty acres, all to no avail. The calf was never found.

We eventually gave up our search. Coming across a cut of sheep on the way back to the settlement, we took them in and selected ten of the best for mutton, our thoughts very much on the events of the afternoon and our fears for the future should any of those events come to light.

At the end of that rather fateful day, Ken invited me to return the revolver to the Boss's house, I declined the invitation, fearing that I might have been asked questions that would have tested my ability to tell the truth. It was one of those occasions when the line between not telling the truth or avoiding telling a lie was very narrow indeed.

When he eventually plucked up courage to return the gun. Mrs. Clements did ask him if "He had done the job OK", and received a mumbled reply which would not have stood up to detailed questioning.

The presence of the calf and the dead cow had originally been reported by some of the children from the settlement. There was nothing whatsoever to stop them seeing it again, if they chose to go riding in that area, which was very likely, even if only out of morbid curiosity. There was also to be a two-night dance at Chartres, just over a week later and a number of people would be travelling that way.

Our abiding fear was that someone would find the calf and start to ask questions, plans had been made to have a dance in the cookhouse on Saturday night, when people from Fox Bay West would ride or drive around rather than come by boat, particularly if the wind was a bit fresh and creating white tops on the waves in the harbour.

The dance came and went. I went upstairs to bed at about 2 a.m. with a much-mellowed attitude and ready for sleep, which was not long in coming. I had not been asleep long, however, when I was disturbed by someone entering my room and from a hazy sleep recognised Ken standing by my bed, dressed, because it was a typically stormy night, in black waterproof trousers, jacket and sou-wester, asking if he could borrow my knife, which was part of the stock-in-trade of any shepherd or roustabout. My immediate reaction was to think that he had elected to cut his own throat rather than take any longer the suspense of being found out but I soon realised that it was unlikely that he would bother to dress himself in waterproof clothing if he were going to inflict upon himself a fatal injury. No, he was going to walk out to the Horse Paddock, in the dead of night, to dispose of the red calf, in so doing remove once and for all, the fear that someone would stumble on our secret. As Ken was to find out, it was not to be an easy task.

Finding a suitable hiding place was in itself difficult. Ken decided that the beach, albeit a good half mile away, was the safest hiding place, even that presented its own problem. It was unlikely that anyone would walk along that particular stretch of shoreline, but unless the carcass was pinned down with rocks, of which there was a marked absence along that part of the beach, it would float away and possibly land up on the beach below the settlement. There seemed no alternative but to make use of the crates that ran out to sea.

The crates were wooden structures, about eight feet square, that ran from the end of a fence where it met the beach to a point below the low tide mark, thus rendering it impossible for the animals, particularly sheep, to escape from one paddock to another when the tide was out. In order to prevent the crates being washed out to sea, it was necessary to fill them with large rocks, many of them requiring more than one man to lift.

The task that Ken had set himself was formidable. The walk from the settlement to the Horse Paddock would take about an hour and carrying the calf from where it lay to the beach required three journeys, with the added problem of first taking all the rocks out of a crate and then replacing them on top of the carcass. He returned about 8.00 a.m., worn out but a little more relaxed. Not surprising, our problems were still not all behind us.

The week preceeding the dance at Chartres was uneventful. Ken and I were going to the dance. The Boss was due back from Dunnose Head on Thursday afternoon. The fear that he may go out of his way to check that we had got rid of the black and white calf, was close to the forefront of our minds. To the best of our knowledge he would be the first person to travel through the Horse Paddock since our day of disasters. Thursday was passing without incident. We saw Mr. Clements ride into the settlement shortly after tea. Work for the day had finished, Ken had gone to collect the paddock mare, who spent most of her day in the settlement. It was usual for farms to have a paddock horse, generally a faithful friend, easy to catch and used for short trips to the paddocks adjacent to the settlement. Shortly after six o'clock, the Foreman, Mike Murphy, came across the green to the cookhouse. "The Boss wants to see you and Ken right away" he said. "He does not seem to have had a particularly good trip", which was a thinly veiled indication that, to say the least, he was not in a very good mood. My heart sank. Ken was not back and Mr. Clements was not likely to be well pleased, if kept waiting, particularly if the subject was the one that Ken and I both feared.

I stalled as long as I dare in the hope that Ken would return. This particular piece of music was, as far as I was concerned, best sung as a duet. Unable to wait any longer, I made my way over to the Boss's gear shed, where I would expect to find him after a long journey. Thankfully I was right first time. Having made the decision to face the problem head on I saw no value in wasting further time. I could only liken it to the condemned man whose last appeal had been turned down, let's get on with it.

He was busy cleaning and waxing his riding gear when I walked in. He looked up momentarily as I entered and with little more than a grunt carried on cleaning his gear. After what seemed like an age he looked up and asked, "Roger, what horses do you want to take to Chartres at the weekend?" Every ounce of strength drained from me. My knees seemed to buckle beneath me, my mind went blank.

If my feelings were like the condemned man losing his last appeal before, now they could only be likened to the same man who found that the trap door had failed to open for the third time.

The relief was devastating. I mumbled some reply about taking my two colts, Tango and Imp, and felt determined to find Ken and express my displeasure at having to face the ordeal on my own.

Two weeks passed before the answer to one of our questions became known. Although the Government personnel used many of the services of the sheep station, they were expected to provide their own milk. Charlie Maddox, the wireless operator, had told both Ken and I that he had lost one of his milking cows, with her calf, a week or so before the fateful day, but it had completely gone from our thoughts, even when racking our minds for an answer to the nagging question of the origin of both cow and calf.

Having realised it some weeks later, we chose to accept that discretion being the better part of valour, we would not reveal the truth. To have done so would have opened a web of intrigue and led to questions that we felt were best left to bubble to the surface in the fullness of time.

CHAPTER 19

ACHILLES HEEL EXPOSED

Ken Spicer and I had agreed to meet at the Hawks Nest shanty the evening before a large gather. As I approached the shanty it was clear that Ken had arrived before me. His horse, Spirit, the large grey mare that had more than matched up to her name some months before, was in the small horse paddock adjacent to the shanty. There was no sign of Ken, which did not surprise me, I would have expected to find him inside lighting a fire or sweeping out the accumulation of dust and dirt that had built up from lack of occupancy for a number of weeks. I tied my horse to the hitching rail and made my way up the two steps and went to open the door. As I did so it was clear that something on the other side was preventing it from opening freely.

My first reaction was to assume that Ken was giving the shanty a long overdue scrub-out. It was quite clear that he was doing something with the furniture as the air was rent with much thumping and bumping, so much so that I was unable to make him hear. It was only when I put my shoulder to the door and pushed sufficiently hard that I was able to move the furniture that had been pushed against the door on the other side that he realised I was there. Too late for him but just in time for me to see him standing on a kitchen chair throwing an accumulation of work boots in the direction of a small, harmless and very frightened field mouse, which had somehow got into the shanty and was now, only too desperately, trying to find a way out. Ken gave a lengthy explanation for his elevated position, the substance of which was that he had climbed onto the chair to get a better view, a tale which I could see no reason to believe, as all the signs pointed to the fact that he was afraid of this, the smallest of creatures, which even now, was making good use of the disruption caused by my entry to escape by making a dash up the side of the open peat fireplace and straight up the chimney, which despite my earlier thoughts, had not been lit.

Ken was protesting angrily at my suggestion of cowardice as we set about putting the furniture straight and gathering up the array of stray boots which had found themselves in every corner of the room. Although sparsely furnished, the long bench-like table and two stools that were more than adequate for our needs were heavy enough to require both of us to put straight. We worked in silence, I being satisfied that I had found a little weakness in his character, he more than a little hurt at the realisation that his protest of innocence was falling on disbelieving ears.

As I lifted my end of the table, my foot came into contact with a boot that had been missed from our earlier collection. It slid across the floor towards where Ken was standing and out ran the offending four legged intruder. With one shout my thirteen stone friend leaped from the floor to the stool and onto the table in two short steps, effectively destroying his defence and putting him in a bad humour for some days to come and added to the series of events that were to beset him. For my part, I was only glad that the mouse did not come my way, it was unlikely that there would have been room on the stool for both of us!

The next morning we rode north to the Little Chartres camp and then west, meeting Mr Clements and the other members of the Fox Bay gang at White Gate Corner, under Mount Philomel. Our intention was, with help from

Bill Paice and young George, to gather up all the sheep in the Narrows camp, take them back to the Gun Hill shanty, where we proposed to separate the ewes from the wethers, to clip the growth of wool from around the eyes of those that were unable to see properly, a necessary task in late winter, to limit the numbers that might fall into the swollen rivers and streams.

After a brief discussion on our proposed programme, Ken broke away from the gather and headed for Gun Hill with the instruction to kill a sheep and prepare an evening meal. The rest of us carried on and about three hours later brought the sheep into the pens around the shanty. Although it was late in the afternoon we pressed on with the eyelocking, not wishing to be away from our own beds back in the settlement any longer than was absolutely necessary. Ken, in the meantime, was getting on with the meal. Smoke was coming out of the chimney and a freshly killed sheep was hanging from the "Blinky". Very few people volunteered for the job of cook when out on gather, even fewer complained about the quality of the end product, otherwise that was about the quickest way of ensuring that you would get the task of cooking the next meal, as anyone could imagine.

There was no oven in the shanty, just an open grate with a small side recess where the kettle was left to stand and keep warm. The cooking was done in a "shadro", best described as a large, round, cast iron pot, which stood on red hot embers, raked out from the fire above. The lid had turned up sides, with a ring in the centre for lifting, upon which more red hot embers were raked, to provide all round cooking and a near perfect way to cook a casserole or stew. "Near perfect", was the right expression, because it did not always work out that way, particularly if the elected cook was either not keen or, as in Ken's case, totally opposed to the job.

That frame of mind was not conducive to a good end result.

Ken's knowledge of cooking was limited to knowing that it required heat, meat, and water. When we eventually went into the shanty to eat it was clear that he had made an honest attempt to prepare a substantial meal. There was bread and margarine on the table, a saucepan of reconstituted powdered potatoes, and a neck of mutton cooking in the shadro.

Five people sat down to eat that evening, four of them secretively, and silently, asking themselves why had Ken selected the neck and shoulder for us to eat? We never ate the neck in the cookhouse, it was more suited for the dogs to chew. Of all the cuts of meat he could have selected it was not only the toughest but took longest to cook. His answer, when eventually asked, was that "It was the first piece I came too", which was difficult to deny.

To say that the meat that evening was tough would have been an understatement, consequently we chewed in silence. Mr Clements was the only one around the table prepared to make any observation, he then restricted it to, "A bit rubbery Ken, but quite tasty". Even as Boss he was not immune from being awarded the job of cook.

Sleeping in the shanty should not be confused with the comparative luxury of cookhouse accommodation. Generally they were two-roomed buildings, one for cooking and eating, the other equipped with bunk beds fitted with thin mattresses, one or two sheepskins and non-interior sprung slatted boards. It was by no means unheard of for a number of the boards to be removed, leaving just enough to retain the mattress and skins, so that when the would-be occupant leapt up to the top bunk, he would find himself back down to the bottom with split-second timing.

When working away from the settlement we were expected to take advantage of all the daylight hours, sleep was therefore important, although sometimes difficult to come by, particularly if one of the occupants in the shanty was inclined to snore when lying on his back, which was very much the case if the Boss was included in the gang. He was inclined to drop off to sleep and start snoring, sufficient to lift the roof, as soon as his head hit the pillow, or to be correct, a rolled up sheepskin. It was therefore, privately, a competition to get into our bunks early, in the hope that sleep came before he turned in. If not our night was likely to be interrupted at frequent intervals, with a series of snorts and whistles, only broken when someone threw a boot across the floor, which was usually sufficient to disturb him and as a result cause him to change his position.

That night in Gun Hill was no different from any other, with the end result that shortly before first light there were a few bleary eyes trying to look fit and full of vigour without making it obvious that one of our number had been solely responsible for everyone else having a disturbed night.

Our temporary cook, unable to lose his job, was left to prepare our breakfast chops, cooked in the shadro, with thick gravy and dried onion rings for additional flavour. It had all the hallmarks of a meal fit for royalty, particularly after the three hours work which we had spent gathering the sheep from the Chartres end of the Gun Hill camp, and penning them ready to be eyelocked after we had eaten.

The aroma that met us as we approached the door was sufficient to dispel any fears about the sincerity of Ken's assurance that he was preparing our food to the best of his ability, it was in that frame of mind that we sat down to eat the entire complement of chops from one full grown sheep. They were delicious and tender, but for some reason, known only to Ken, every mouthful was covered with a fine grit, a texture like undissolved salt. No one dared to ask why. With puzzled expressions passing between the gang we ate on. It was Ken himself who eventually made the observation, by way of an admission, that he had experienced a small accident when checking to see that the chops were cooking to his satisfaction. He had correctly lifted the heavy lid from the shadro, by the ring in the centre, but had forgotten to first rake off the accumulation of fine ash from around the edge, with the consequence that about two handfuls of fine ash had fallen into the chops, it was his hope that they would have dissolved in the gravy leaving us none the wiser, unfortunately that was not to be. It was easy to say that we were expected to take the rough with the smooth, but sometimes it was a little difficult to see the smooth when surrounded by so much rough.

HAWKSNEST SHANTY.

CHAPTER 20

THOSE WE HAVE MET

Towards the end of the season, I gave notice of my intention to leave Fox Bay and go into Stanley, hoping to find work there or on the boats working in and around the islands, wishing to put both sheep and associated work behind me for a while, believing that it would not be long before I returned home to England.

I had only been in town for a few days, staying as I had done on previous visits, with Carrie McLeod. She had heard my name announced over the local radio as being on the passenger list for the aircraft the next day, and had prepared a bed for me, anticipating that I would soon be walking up across the green. When I had a telephone call from the island's Civil Engineer inviting me to attend his office for an interview, it transpired that there was a job available on the West Falklands, which required operating heavy land drainage equipment. He wondered if I might be interested in it. I agreed and prepared to go back to the West Falklands which I had left only a few days before believing at the time for good. A number of reasons had prompted me to accept the job when offered, not least of which was a handsome increase in salary.

The Falkland Island Government had a responsibility to improve, wherever possible, the island's natural resources, one such area was land drainage and track improvement between individual farms. I already knew the principal equipment operator and it was with him that I would be working.

William Ferguson, known as Jock, was a Scot and a canny one at that. He had arrived in the Colony some months before and I had got to know him well. It was primarily at his request that I was offered the job.

The equipment on which I would be second operator was a Cuthbertson Albion Water Buffalo and a Massey-Ferguson bulldozer. The Buffalo was a massive vehicle which was eight feet high, twelve feet long, and nine feet wide, six of which was track, making it possible to travel almost anywhere and particularly on the waterlogged peat bogs that resulted in so much poor vegetation. It never ceased to amaze me that in spite of its weight and size it was able to travel with ease over, what was in effect a shimmering swamp and which would have been impossible to walk on without sinking knee deep.

I had a few days to spare before flying back to the camp. It was an opportunity to be a part of a different community, but still very much a part of what I considered to be precious and was already a very important part of my life. The island people asked for no more than simplicity of style and possessions, and expected no more than what was right.

It was possible to see in every islander a sense of purpose and the need for other people. For many of us, life was not just richer "for having lived", the real jewel in the crown was "for having lived there", sharing in so many of its interests and activities.

Once again there was an opportunity to reflect not only on the environment within which we lived but also on our colleagues and acquaintances and from them recognise the characters whose contribution to a way of life stood out and became well known, if not renowned, within the Colony. In being themselves they left an indelible mark on those privileged to be known as their friends.

Doug Christian was one such individual, well known for his reluctance to do his washing on even a semi-regular basis, preferring to buy new socks, a dozen at a time, until his wardrobe was quite literally full to overflowing. Even then, no amount of coaxing, threats or offers to stoke up the boiler for him would bring the desired result until he had been through them yet again and worn them all for a second time, still unwashed. When Doug did give in, generally only after the intervention of the station Boss, every clothes line available was pressed into service. Without fear of exaggeration the wash would include some forty pairs of socks and almost as many shirts and sets of underwear. His annual winter holiday to visit his mother was largely at her insistence and marked by the inclusion of large volumes of dirty washing, identified and paid for as excess baggage on the aircraft passenger list.

Doug was also well known for his short tempered manner, which manifested itself not only at odd moments but when it was least expected. One occasion in particular was when he was engaged, with others, in carrying out minor repairs to the roof of a house in the settlement. He had the misfortune to strike his thumb with a hammer and flying into a fit of rage, he threw the hammer as far and as hard as he could before climbing down the ladder to go and have the injured thumb bandaged, an operation that took some time. On his return, having climbed all the way back up the ladder, he inquired after his hammer, only to be told that it was exactly where he had thrown it some time before - an observation which immediately sent him into a second bout of bad temper.

A brief skirmish one Saturday afternoon left Doug with a cut lip and a twisted ankle, the latter sustained when he slipped on a chop bone discarded by one of the dogs. The incident came to the attention of the station Manager who chose to see both men involved, secretly knowing full well how the injury to Doug's ankle had come about. He chose to ask, by way of introducing the subject of the altercation, how it had happened, which brought the near-tearful reply: "I was trying to bloody well fight and I couldn't".

The camp on the opposite side of the Philomel Pass and immediately opposite the Dunnose Head settlement was owned by the Falkland Island Company and managed from Fox Bay West. Known as Spring Point, it had at one time been a modest settlement and subsequently looked after by one old shepherd, reputed to be the son of the last pirate to plague the remote islands. He stole sheep which he then took to Chile and Patagonia and fur seals, already a protected species, now only found in sizeable quantities on the remote islands of Steeple Jason to the north- west of the two main islands.

The old shepherd would sometimes bring our mail from Fox Bay and place it in the mail box located on the "Point", overlooking the harbour, for that purpose. In order to attract our attention to its presence - it was three quarters of a mile away - he would light a fire from diddle-dee twigs and driftwood from the beach, which Two Bob Skilling could easily see when standing in his usual place by the large wooden sink in the galley. He, in his turn, would hasten to where we were working to acquaint us of this major event to which we responded by taking the first opportunity to row over and collect it, as usual an eagerly awaited event.

Known simply as "Old Charlie", my most memorable recollection of him was at an annual sports gathering at Port Howard where he had taken up temporary lodgings in an old army bell tent - not the one with tiny holes in the side about twelve inches off the ground - erected especially for the occasion. Sharing the tent with him was a contemporary by the name of Bill Tyler. Both gentlemen had taken custody of ample supplies of refreshment. Towards the end of the week, Old Charlie was sitting alone outside the tent. There was no visible sign of Bill. Enquiry as to the whereabouts of his partner brought the slow characteristic reply, "Ah, Bill and me have teamed up. I drink's his whisky and he goes to sleep".

Our shepherd Boss, which was his rightful title, in Fox Bay East was Sue Binnie, an uncommonly quiet spoken, Gentle-man, who was never known to smoke, drink or use bad language. Dang or heck were the most common adjectives he would use when sufficiently angered to speak out, even then it was his dogs that were most likely to have provoked him. Sue, with his wife Rosie, never ventured far from the farm. When asked on one occasion why he didn't go into Stanley for a holiday from time to time, he responded by saying: "I went there once, I have all I need here at home". Home was an isolated cottage, an hour's ride from the settlement, known as Blue Mountain, on the track to Port Howard.

One of the West Falkland's most respected residents was Mrs "Mac" who, with her husband Jack, lived for most, if not all of her working life, at Goring House, close to where the track between Fox Bay and Chartres crossed the Chartres River. Goring House was the point at which all the telephone lines on the West came together. Mrs "Mac" was the official but unpaid operator, a post that she held since the introduction of the telephone and only gave up when more modern (not to be confused with high technology) equipment made her job unnecessary. For her service to the community, she was later awarded the Order of the British Empire.

It was in the home of Jack and Mrs "Mac", as they were affectionately known, that I first experienced the hospitality of an outside shepherd, and realised afterwards as I rode away the depth of offence I would have caused had I ridden straight by. Like so many of their contemporaries, they lived their lives to the full, wanting nothing, lacking nothing. The menfolk would ride into the settlement for stores about once a month for a visit often lasting no more than a hour. The womenfolk often did not venture into the settlement for one, two or three years at a time.

In the camp, no attempt was made to set aside either Sunday or religious festivals as being anything different from another day off, whereas in Stanley much of the social life, limited as it was to whist drives and dances, was under the auspices of the established churches, principally the Roman Catholic Church of St. Mary on Ross Road, painted in its almost traditional green and white, the colour probably influenced by its Irish Priest, the Reverend Monsignor Ireland. Further along the road was the unmistakeable Christ Church Cathedral, inescapable from the first impression, and an everlasting memory. Playing an equally important role in the community was the Presbyterian Tabernacle in Barrack Street, led by the Reverend Forrest McWhan. A small group of people supporting the Bahai faith had quietly gone about their work in Stanley, for more years than most residents of the town cared to remember.

Undoubtedly there was a loyal and devout following for all the Churches but equally outstanding was the large number of people who had perhaps spent most of their lives on the farms of the East and West Falklands, who viewed the mystique that surrounded the Church with suspicion and apprehension and were more than wary of any association with it. In the camp the two principal ceremonies of marriage and funerals were presided over by the Farm Manager who assumed the role of Registrar, taking all that was necessary from a book, often with little regard for the possibility that the participating parties, either dead or alive, may have followed a particular faith.

For the dead, each settlement had its own small cemetery surrounded by a picket fence to keep out the sheep, although they were let in from time to time to keep the grass down. Coffins were made when required by the handyman in the Carpenters shop with both care and consideration. The only ceremony was at the graveside, with a few words taken from the Prayer Book, it was then customary for the gang to be given the rest of the day off as a mark of respect.

The Police Force consisted of just three locally-recruited officers, with the Police Chief, regarded as the professional, brought from the United Kingdom, and crime detection was largely by instinct and gut feeling. Of the more serious crime, petty theft was the most common, probably the majority of that from ships. Living in a close knit community like Stanley, theft by adults from neighbours and kinsmen was uncommon.

Although the roads were poorly maintained and in total only about twenty miles, most of the offences requiring Police attention, were for motoring misdemeanours such as excessive speed within the town, or for poorly maintained vehicles. A surprising number of residents owned cars and Land Rovers and there were a number of vans, lorries and tractors required for the onshore transport of goods.

The traditional policy of crime prevention, rather than crime detection after the event, was a much encouraged intention.

Working in such a small community and being drawn from within their own number meant that the officers not only knew the inhabitants as family and friends, they also had to live with them.

When punishment was required, the Offender knew that everyone would get to hear about it. News, particularly of an unsavoury nature, travelled fast. If it was not included as an item for broadcast in the weekly news, it would not escape transmission by word of mouth.

Regardless of our origin, whether it was the United Kingdom or the

Falkland Islands, excessive drinking was the biggest potential danger. The particularly long winter evenings, without organised activities or leisure pursuits readily available, encouraged boredom. Fortunately, card playing for money was banned, not to have been would have encouraged increased crime, someone always has to lose. It was easy to see, with hindsight, that the single men in particular were in a make or break situation. On the large stations a regular round of drinking could be expected most weekends. The inhabitants could be divided into three groups, some were always there, some were there occasionally, the remainder, which was also the minority, were never there.

The Blacklist was a form of control for those who drank to excess and in doing so got into trouble or made a nuisance of themselves. It prohibited the Offender from drinking, buying or being given, either ashore or afloat, any intoxicant, anywhere in the Islands. Those found supplying could expect to receive a similar penalty.

The list inevitably included the names of single men who, having worked hard for two or three years, on an outlying sheep farm, came into town for an extended winter holiday for two or three months, then, having been unable to stand the pace found themselves before the Court, to receive the "Ultimate Accolade", for the following twelve months. For many, it mattered not one bit. Once sober, they were ready to go back to the camp and the routine of work.

The Blacklist provided little help for the heavy or habitual drinkers who were frequently drunk but never made a nuisance of themselves.

The Court in Stanley was presided over by a Stipendiary Magistrate. Minor matters and those that called for short custodial sentence were dealt with quickly. Serious matters calling for Judge and Jury, were transferred to the United Kingdom, finding twelve jurors who would not have known

Defendant would have been a near impossibility.

I went to Court one day, for no other reason than to pass the time. Included in the Court business was a matter concerning one Don Banks. He was charged that on the previous day he had been found drunk, to which he pleaded guilty, and asked that his statement to the Arresting Officer be offered in mitigation.

Don stood in the dock, with the hint of a smile on his face, already having a very good idea of the outcome. A fine would have been out of the question. The Officer read the statement, which was to the effect that, when asked why his eyes were glazed, his speech slurred and his reason for hanging on so firmly to a picket fence - outside the Police Station - Don replied that he was suffering from "Demerara". A ripple of laughter sounded around the Court. It was clear that Don was unaware that Demerara was the name given to a particular type of sugar but it was well known that it was the name of a very popular beverage, rum. A closer definition of the condition from which he was suffering would, in all probability, be difficult to find. The circumstances made his condition, as he had stated it, most likely to be true. The Officer went on to explain that on further questioning Don had meant to say that he was suffering from dermatitis and the pills prescribed by the doctor had accelerated the condition. The Magistrate, deciding that Don's first declaration of the reason for his condition was most likely to be the correct one, duly instructed that his name be placed on the Blacklist for a period of twelve months.

The situation in the camp was quite different, with only one source of alcohol in each settlement. The Company-run store opened for just a short period each Saturday, about mid-day. In settlements where the store did open during the week it would certainly exclude the sale of drink. The purchase of alcohol was limited to one bottle of spirits and twelve bottles of beer, or its equivalent. Regardless of circumstances, to report for work under the influence of drink would result in instant dismissal.

Naturally, married men were not immune from the occasional drinking spree, often to the consternation of the "little woman" who became like a raving tiger when "hubby fell off the wagon".

One memorable occasion emanated from an annual two night dance at an adjacent West Falkland farm. While waiting for the second night of dancing to begin, and very much suffering from the effects of the first, I and a fellow sufferer went visiting taking with us, largely untouched, a bottle of whisky, which to any participant in an annual two nighter, was the only ingredient necessary for an event looking for somewhere to happen.

Much of the residual discomfort from the previous night was beginning to recede as we made our second call. The lady of the house was herself out visiting, which with hindsight, was undoubtedly to our advantage. Our host invited us to come in and sit down, adding the cautionary note that we must be quiet as his small child was asleep in the next room.

Three glasses were quickly brought and as we sat chatting it became clear that our Host was also suffering from the previous night's jollifications and welcomed a glass of our own particular brand of pain reliever. For almost an hour, over our one drink we told tales of misfortune that had befallen absent colleagues and acquaintances, by which time the driving force of this particular household had returned. The frosty stare was more than sufficient to convey the message that any incautious remark could herald the need for a quick departure. It was under that umbrella we continued to talk and ignored the bottle and empty glasses standing on the table.

Having allowed a discreet period of time to elapse, as a prelude to leaving, my colleague, who insisted much later that he was only trying to be polite, made the unfortunate mistake of inviting our host to have one last drink. He hesitated before declining, then slowly added, "I think I am going to be unwell". It was a remark sufficient to goad the little lady into action, it was such a reaction that resulted in our host making a dive for the bathroom, closely followed by the lady, clearly lacking understanding and concern for his well being.

We chose that same moment to leave, clearing the stile that led to the road and cookhouse in two short strides, congratulating ourselves on our narrow escape and grateful for the diversion that made it possible.

Although full modernisation of the plumbing facilities was still some way off, many homes, particularly those in the larger settlements, had hot and cold running water, the former being heated in a peat burning Rayburn cooker. Fresh water was obtained by damming a convenient stream and either by pump or gravity, feed it into a large holding tank from where it could be fed into the homes. Modern flush toilets were evident in many of the houses in the settlement from where all household waste was channelled, just below the surface of the ground to a point on the beach a few feet beyond low tide, where the continual washing of the beach by the incoming and outgoing tide took the waste out to sea. Unattractive as it may appear, it was a rewarding place to catch mullet.

Toilet facilities for homes without running water were very much like those in villages and small hamlets in the UK in the 1950s, where the toilet was a small wooden shed at the bottom of the garden and its contents emptied by the Council refuse cart. We were much more fortunate in the islands. Most of the time we had a constant supply of water to our smallest room, particularly at high tide. The outward appearance of the toilet was identical to those in the UK, the principal difference was that ours were built on twelve foot stilts about twenty feet out from the edge of the beach, which ensured that the toilet was flushed at least twice a day by the incoming tide. Another feature that set it apart was that in order to reach it a long narrow bridge was necessary, which could be best described as being complete with its own private jetty.

With winds over twenty knots, going to the toilet could frequently be considered a hazardous experience. More often than not, sitting jauntily at an acute angle, the result of countless buffeting gales, any visitor unable to wait for the gale to abate was obliged to brace himself by wedging his feet firmly against the door in front and at the same time seek support with outstretched arms on either side. The request to "come and look for me if I'm not back in ten minutes" was taken seriously, particularly at high tide, when a call to the most inexpensive bidet in the world was necessary. A good number were known to break away from their elevated perch during inclement weather, fortunately most were unoccupied, which was more by good luck than good management.

CHAPTER 21

FISH ON THE MENU

Leaving Stanley for my new land drainage job, we took off from the slipway close by the Government hanger which was about a mile to the west of town. Our route was to take us to the North Arm settlement on the East Falklands where we were to take the only other passenger on the flight. With that part of our journey accomplished we headed for Port Howard but this time it was not our intention to land. Our plan on this and other calls that afternoon was to deliver mail which, under normal circumstances, would have waited until the need arose for the aircraft to take passengers. However, on this occasion, the flight that we were on was to be the last before a major refit which would take the Beaver aircraft out of service for about ten days. There was nothing more frustrating for people living in the camp than knowing that there was mail in Stanley waiting for an opportunity to be delivered - so near and yet so far away.

Mail drops were a common experience. The aircraft flew in low over a settlement to attract the attention of the resident, making sure that someone would be on hand to see where the package fell. Some months earlier, while on a similar mission, to New Island, the resident failed to observe where the much anticipated mail fell, which resulted in it remaining undetected for three weeks and caused considerable upset to all concerned. Usually only letters would be delivered in this way, the total package weighing about two pounds, sufficient for it to be seen and yet not too heavy so as to cause injury should the recipient find himself too close for comfort. The other downside of this form of delivery was that the package could bounce two or three times and be lost in the long grass, or wherever else it happened to fall, as was the case on New Island. There was however no such misfortune on this occasion. The mail, thrown clear of the aircraft, bounced two or three times on the short grass and was clearly visible. We made a return run to acknowledge the cheery wave from the ground which signalled the safe recovery, banked sharply and turned inland before heading west towards Hill Cove and another drop.

A bit bored by the monotony of flying at the usual twelve to fifteen hundred feet the pilot, Jim Kerr, decided that it was an ideal day for practising his crop-spraying technique, an occupation he had enjoyed before taking up his appointment as second pilot in the colony.

It was most certainly a new experience for me as we descended to a mere thirty feet, travelling at one hundred and forty miles an hour. The undulating countryside interspersed with long flat peat bogs, covered in coarse white grass, often surrounded by sand banks, also made it an exhilarating experience as the miles sped by. We repeated our earlier procedure for the mail drop at Hill Cove and turned back inland, this time flying south east, to Fox Bay and my destination, where I expected to be met by Jock Ferguson.

Although I was flying to Fox Bay, it was our intention to leave immediately for Chartres, where we were going to spend some months maintaining the two tractors and draining some of the waterlogged pieces of camp around the settlement. It was comforting to see the Fox Bay settlement from the air. It had played an important part in my life and an aerial view placed it into an all-embracing perspective. The red roofed houses contrasting against the brilliant white walls, it was good to be back.

Jock had bought the Buffalo through from Chartres and the reason soon became clear. His own living accommodation had been completed and he was determined to take it back with us. His pride and joy, which he was to share with his wife Jean, was a caravan about twenty feet long. It had been built in Fox Bay by Mike Murphy and by any standard it was superb, built on skids that ran its entire length. Its interior was finished in panelled board which, with its cupboards and furniture, was equal to the same high standards expected in professionally built mobile homes. The test of workmanship was to be displayed many times when moving from one site to another. Not once did it prove necessary to pack away any of the kitchen-ware or crockery which, when considering the rough terrain over which it was drawn, was little short of a miracle. The only difficulty encountered was getting it moving. A normal caterpillar tractor was never able to move it, the length, width and consequently the weight saw to that.

We arrived at Chartres without incident. Although there was a smaller caravan for me to use, it seemed sensible to have a room in the cookhouse and eat there when appropriate, which during the winter months was most of the time. I, of course, knew most of the lads who lived and worked there, having visited the settlement many times when I worked at Dunnose Head and Fox Bay East. It was the Chartres Manager, Keith Luxton, who had established the link with the agent in my home village, and through whom so many young men were recruited. It was, therefore, not surprising that we had many things in common. Unbelievable as it may seem, there was one occasion, at a dance in the cookhouse, when ten of us had all attended the same school back home in England.

For part of my stay, the cook at Chartres was Bernard Christian whose mood changed with each passing day of the week. From Monday until Friday it was impossible to engage him in conversation. A civil word would rarely pass his lips until Saturday morning at breakfast time. Then he might have ventured to suggest that the weekend looked like being fine or that it could be a good weekend for fishing off the end of the jetty. At coffee time mid-morning he would be all smiles and laughter. It was not in itself the prospect of a pleasant weekend or a break from the endless preparation of meals that brought about the transformation, but the approaching store time, when in addition to buying the cookhouse groceries, he had the opportunity to replenish his wine cabinet, which had remained empty, since the previous weekend.

Because of the need to obtain provisions for the cookhouse, the cook was permitted to do all his shopping before lunch. The rest of the station staff had to wait until mid-afternoon. The early visit to the store ensured that by lunch time Bernard was all smiles and eager to strike up a conversation, in-between regular visits to his room, which was downstairs and led directly off the mess.

By the time lunch was finished Bernard was so affable that he had little difficulty in coaxing someone to help him with the washing up which, once complete, would see him adjourn to his room for a restful afternoon. By supper time he could barely stand, it was between that state and total oblivion that he remained for the entire weekend, with turn-to time on Monday morning finding him back to the usual state of being totally disagreeable.

The practice came to an abrupt end at six o'clock one Monday morning when the men reporting for work revealed that there was no sign of the cook, consequently no early morning coffee. Mr Luxton saw it as a totally unacceptable state of affairs, as would any other farm manager. He immediately left the shearing shed to investigate the whereabouts of the cook, a mission that quickly bore fruit, which resulted in Bernard being dismissed with one month's notice. Had there been another cook readily available it surely would have been a minutes notice. Although still a long way from a state of sobriety, he was able to recognise that he was still in considerable difficulty. Breakfast was a little more than an hour away and sixteen men would be looking for a wholesome meal, sufficient to sustain them for the next four hours. Clearly something had to be arranged, and fast.

At exactly one minute past eight, the entire gang arrived for breakfast, not being quite sure what to expect. It was no secret that the cook had been fired. The spread which met their eyes was truly original. A large loaf of bread stood at each end of the long trestle table, down each side were eight gleaming white plates, and on each stood a fourteen ounce tin of McCray kippered herrings, unopened. But resting on the top of each one was the metal key used to strip back the lid.

Much of those early weeks were spent improving the track between the top cookhouse and the Chartres settlement. We bulldozed off the top soil from a clay ridge and filled the resulting cavity with finely crushed rock, to give not only a firm surface, but one that was smooth and well drained. The road took us down to a wide stream over which was a strong wooden bridge. It was while we were taking a close look at the approach to the bridge that Jock saw a large fish leap clear of the water. Surprise of all surprises. We had discovered four and five pound trout coming up the freshwater stream to spawn. It was well known that small fish had been introduced to a number of streams in the islands, but these mature fish were the first to be discovered on the West. A closer and more careful search revealed that the stream was full of many potential meals.

My canny Scottish colleague was more than determined to be the first to have one on his dinner plate. He lay down on the short cropped grass of the river bank and gently put his hand deep into the water and under the bank. Within seconds a handsome trout lay on the bank and Jock was looking for more to join it. In the centre of the wide but comparatively shallow stream was a large flat rock, the top of which stood just clear of the water and sufficiently wide enough for both of us to stand and guddle for fish. My only knowledge of fishing had been gained with a garden cane and a bent pin on the end of a piece of string. This was a totally new and exciting experience, despite taking some time to catch my first trout.

The trick, at which Jock was more than experienced, was to gently run a hand in the shallow water until he felt the underside of the fish resting close to the edge. Moving carefully forward until the thumb and forefinger were close to the opening gills, a sharp upward flick of the wrist would bring the trout flying through the air and onto the bank. Clearly he had caught fish this way many times before.

Like two overgrown kids, we ran from one side of the river to the other, determined to catch sufficient for the entire Chartres settlement to benefit from our morning's sport. It was while we were thus engaged that the doctor, making a leisurely return to Fox Bay from Hill Cove where he had been for the previous two days, happened to come across this tranquil scene, as he was later to describe it, although in reality it was far from tranquil. The doctor was a Yorkshireman and perfectly able to recognise a good fish when he saw one and joined in willingly. Fortunately it was a warm day with no more than a good breeze blowing, which was lessened by the small rounded hills that sheltered the valley, through which the river ran. We were greeted in the settlement with surprise and considerable excitement, each home it seemed perfecting numerous ways in which to cook trout. Fried, poached, baked and stuffed all were tried, with varying degrees of success.

The method used to catch our fish was, of course, quite illegal and word gradually spread until one day, some two or three weeks after we had made our original discovery, we received a telegram from the Colonial Secretary, effectively our Boss, but also custodian of the birds of the air and the fish of the sea, which he claimed extended into the rivers and streams. The communication advised us of certain irregularities that had been brought to his notice and we, as Government employees, should know better, or words to that effect. The gist of his telegram instructed us to cease fishing forthwith with the added postscript that, before we did, two of the best fish be put on the first available flight to Stanley, marked for his personal and immediate attention.

When we moved away from the settlement with our caravans, I received one major benefit, for the first time for some months my meals were to be cooked by a woman. Although we had to buy all of our provisions from the station store, like everyone else - our meat was free by courtesy of the farm on which we were working - it did inevitably mean that we would have more tinned vegetables and fruit, luxuries readily dispensed with in the cookhouse.

The benefit did however have one or two short comings, Jeanie had much more than an unfailing ability to overcook a roast of mutton which, when supported by baked beans in tomato sauce and reconstituted potato, provided little encouragement to look forward to the next meal. Frequently the excitement and the anticipation of what the next meal would bring, rested solely on the fervent desire to find the little cube of bacon, secreted in the tin of baked beans by the manufacturer, as part of an advertising campaign. Little could the factory overlords have realised how much hope of finding, was balanced against the despair of losing, in that tiny part of God's Kingdom.

Jock and I decided one day that we would take possession of one of the lambs that were grazing immediately outside the caravan door, but alas, that was not to be. We tried every available method to bring one within our grasp all to no avail. Firstly we tried to out-run it, a method that was doomed to failure, principally because the lamb had four legs to itself, while we only had four between the two of us. We then tried the lasso, and, with Jeanie protesting at having to take in the washing prematurely, it only served to distract us still further from the job in hand. We finally resorted to the use of a .22 calibre rifle which too had to be abandoned. Past experience had proved us incapable of shooting a hole through a tin can that was standing on a gatepost, which reduced our chances of shooting a fast moving, leaping, twisting lamb to zero. Mutton remained the principal dish on the menu, supported by its all too frequent portion of baked beans.

I continued to enjoy roast mutton, but my liking for beans disappeared abruptly one day when our meal was interrupted by the pet cat who, not wishing to be left out of the pleasure of eating, made its protests in the usual way. This prompted the hostess to remove from the cupboard a tin of food which, when opened, was given to the cat. It was a very expensive tin of the best red salmon available, the likes of which, in any form, I had not had the pleasure of eating, or indeed seeing, within the preceding four years.

CHAPTER 22

SHIFTING, SHIMMERING PEAT

I learnt, rather forcibly one afternoon, that the power of our equipment and the resourcefulness of its operators should never be underestimated.

We had been draining some shallow peat flats to the North of Rat Castle shanty. Our caravans were parked near the Green Hill bridge and quite close to the Port Howard settlement. Our chosen route back at the end of the day took us by the Plain House, home of an outside shepherd, Claude Molkenbuhr. Claude, a Chilean by birth, was one of a very small number who lived in the islands and his home was a welcome stopping place for coffee and a chat. Early one evening, following one such respite from our labours, Jock decided to drive on ahead in the Land Rover while I followed with the Buffalo and plough.

There were still three hours of daylight left when we bid goodbye to our host and set out for home. Jock was almost out of sight by the time I had climbed up onto the tractor and got it started. Although the Land Rover was much faster, it also had a far greater distance to travel. The ability of the Buffalo to stay on top of the most waterlogged swamp meant that I could drive in a straight line for the next gate, in so doing cut miles off the conventional route, a feature that was particularly useful, because right outside the Plain House, directly in my path, was a very deep and wet peat bog. So wet in fact that water stood on the surface but still within the capacity of the tractor, the exceptionally wide tracks of which enabled it to stay on top without breaking through the surface, unless of course you happened to be towing a large plough, which I was. It was equally clear that I had forgotten it was there. At least I had until we were about fifty yards across the bog when I felt the tractor starting to labour. A glance over the shoulder provided most, if not all, the answers. The plough was sinking lower and lower into the swamp. As it did so the cutting edge quickly cut into the peat, taking with it not only the carriage but, the tractor as well. Once the tracks broke the surface, it quite literally sank, stern first, into one of the wettest and deepest peat bogs one would expect to find anywhere.

Had it been possible to continue I would have done so but when the tracks, which had previously stood about four feet above the ground, sank out of the sight firmly locked into a sea of peat, I was forced to stop. From that moment I was unable to move forward or back.

With all visible signs suggesting that I had lost about fifty thousand pounds worth of equipment in an extremely short space of time and with the minimum of inconvenience.   I hurried back to the Plain House where, fortunately, there was a telephone. I was greeted with stunned silence by the host who had wished us goodnight only minutes before and had subsequently stood in the doorway watching the drama unfold. I made my call into the settlement, explaining briefly what had happened, and asked for someone to ride out to the caravans and tell Jock, who had still not reached home himself. It was clearly going to be two hours before he could get back to view my handiwork, and more than sufficient time within which I could convince myself that two major pieces of equipment were unlikely to bubble to the surface ever again. The financial consideration was one thing, the replacement, even if possible, did not bear thinking about. At the very minimum it would have taken six months from purchase to arrival in the Colony.

I made my way back out to the bog, unable to remain idle while waiting for Jock to return. I did what I could to separate the two pieces of equipment. The drawbar and the hitch were at least two feet below the surface. With the aid of the trench spade that was always carried on the tractor, I tried to dig away the peat that had boiled up around it, a task made more difficult by the water that replaced each spadeful. Swamp water was never warm, but with the end of the day clearly in sight it was freezing cold as I stood on the submerged framework of the plough, trying to locate the draw-pin that held the tractor and plough together. I knew that it would be impossible to get both pieces out while they were still coupled together, even if rescue was not to be I could at least say I tried. Having located the pin, at arms length beneath the peaty sludge, I gave it a firm twist and pulled. Much to my surprise the two pieces parted. Clearly the wet peat had found its way into the coupling and acted as a lubricant, which was the first piece of good news that had entered into my life within the previous hour or so.

While I stood there, wet and cold, pondering my next move, the Land Rover came into sight over the ridge and around the edge of the bog. Oh how I wished I had taken that route. We would both have been secure in the warmth of our portable homes by now, free of care and anxiety, an emotion that was far removed from my feelings at that moment.

Jock got out of the Rover and walked to where the tractor was firmly entrenched, his face expressionless. Not saying a word, he walked in a complete circle around our pride and joy, staring at it for some seconds, then quite characteristically, rubbed his nose with the back of his hand and allowed a broad grin to spread across his face. The silence was broken by his never-to-be-forgotten words. "We'll never see her bogged like this again in a thousand years, I must go and get my camera". It was my turn to be short and crisp as I snapped back by way of reply that I had been worrying my guts out for nearly two hours, when all he could do was to take bloody photographs.

He slapped me firmly on the back, laughed and said, "I'll take my photos and within five minutes we'll have her out on solid ground, and then we'll take some more". Who was I to disagree, after all no one was to be more relieved than me were he to be proved correct, and correct he was.

Photographs taken for posterity, he drove the Land Rover to the edge of the bog in line with the front of the tractor, securing it firmly with a stout chain around a rock embedded in the ground at the front and ground anchors at the rear, calling out to me as he did so to pay out the cable from the winch that was built into the front of the Buffalo. Having satisfied himself that all that could be done to ensure security had been done, dismissed my slow shake of the head and expressions of doubt with no more than a laugh. He climbed into the driving seat and started the engine, but rather than attempt to drive out as I had anticipated, he put the winch into gear, increased the engine speed as the cable tightened, then winched the bog-bound vehicle to the surface like a phantom monster, almost vertical at first because of the acute angle at which she had been submerged, then levelled out, perfectly capable of being driven away from what had seemed to me to be a peat-ridden grave of indeterminate depth.

Once clear, the tractor was quickly put to work. The drainage plough was still firmly entrenched, in many ways in a worse position than the tractor, mainly because it had heavy steel wheels whereas the tractor was fitted with wide tracks to support it, the plough too, still suspended in its cradle, had sunk to a depth that only the main suspension beam was exposed. Obviously, if it was to come out at all, it would have be the reverse to which it went in. Unlike the tractor, the plough had cut deep into the peat and was unable to go forward.

We dug down yet again to find the low point on which to secure the winch cable, a requirement guaranteed not to raise the temperature in the wellington boots any more than about two degrees above freezing, in spite of the physical effort required. We eventually managed to secure the cable to the stout axle support but it took all the power of the Buffalo with its winch in the lowest gear possible, to break the plough free of the suction holding it in the bog, drawing it back on to firm ground.

Such an experience was not conducive to rest and relaxation, the passage of time between an inevitable disaster and a non-event was but a few hours. It was difficult to comprehend that the episode was all behind me and without cost, reassurance only coming with the passage of time, a very stiff drink and the comfort of my caravan, the small peat burning stove in the corner giving out an all-embracing warmth, even the oil lamp seemed to glow brighter than usual.

The pressurised, oil-burning mantle lamp had many advantages over its contemporary, with a wick, glass funnel and globe. Even in the larger settlements, very few houses had electricity, of those that did most had small individual generators, similar to the one that I had encountered in Fox Bay West, soon after my arrival. Even then, the light flickered continuously, and without batteries to store power it was necessary for the generator to run all the time light was needed.

Port Howard was one of the first settlements to install a generator large enough to provide electricity for most of its houses, unlike the small generators which started up when a light was turned on. It was timed to operate for a given period, depending upon the time of year, usually shutting down at 11 p.m. Notable exceptions were at Christmas time or when a dance or similar function was being held in the cookhouse, which was usually the only building with a room of sufficient size to hold thirty or forty people. Like most man-made pieces of equipment, breakdowns and malfunctions were not uncommon. When the unexpected happened, all thoughts turned to machinery rather than people.

Both the wireless receiver and the radio transmitter drew their source of power from twelve-volt batteries, similar to those used in a car. Of course, they needed to be recharged at regular intervals. Although motorised generators were available in most of the large settlements, regular use was made of small windchargers standing about eight feet high and erected on the top of very strong box-like structures in which were housed the batteries being charged. The stand had to be particularly strong to withstand the almost continuous buffeting of the wind and the force created by the rotating propellor which was six feet in diameter. Even then the windcharger was likely to be smashed to pieces and wrenched from its stand if it were to operate in winds exceeding twenty knots, which often meant that it was impossible to recharge the batteries for as much as a week at a time.

A few months after my experience with the tractor and plough in the peat bog, during what was to be my last Christmas in the Falklands, a large group of people had met together in one house to welcome in the New Year with traditional style. The room was hardly large enough to hold the assembled gathering, so crowded in fact that falling down was improbable but not impossible. I positioned myself in a corner, close to the door and out of harm's way, with only sufficient room to lift my glass, which was conveniently replenished at regular intervals as bottle after bottle was passed around. At a few minutes to midnight the hubbub and noise died down, as most eyes made attempts to focus on the clock hanging above the mantlepiece. No one, it seems, noticed my knees start to buckle under the weight of beverage I had consumed, later reported to have been considerable. I gradually sank, unnoticed, to the floor. I went unnoticed because as I slid down the wall I turned out the only light in the house that was on at that precise moment.

Pandemonium broke loose as frantic calls were made for matches to light candles and oil lamps, always left ready in case of emergencies such as this. Amid the confusion, our host, Victor Summers, and other semi-sober menfolk, made their way out of the house and towards the generator house about two hundred yards away, without giving as much as a second thought to the possibility that the problem could be elsewhere. So intent were they on their mission that they failed to notice that other houses in the settlement still had lights on. It was only as they approached the generator house and could still hear it running perfectly that they started to question the reason for the absence of light. By this time the folk remaining in the house, having become accustomed to the light from the oil lamp, noticed my reclining form in the corner just below the light switch and the truth of the matter dawned. The melee, confusion and eventual conclusion took some minutes, sufficient to make us miss the stroke of midnight and the arrival of the new year.

I remained relatively unpopular for some time after that night and received many assurances that had it not been for the convivial atmosphere prevailing at the time I would most surely have been invited to walk the short plank off the end of the jetty.

In spite of moments of high drama, life generally went on at a slow methodical pace, the future always included more of the same. It was difficult to imagine that the islands could ever be considered home. To have returned to England less than five years from starting my voyage of discovery would have implied failure, which was not something I was prepared to admit or accede to but with a fourth Christmas behind me, I could make plans to return home, before the onset of another winter with its short days and long nights, both dominated by wind and rain.

The Falklands interlude was not over when I boarded the Dutch cargo vessel the *AES* at Port Howard for the overnight journey to Stanley, perhaps the interlude would never be over. My love for the islands and its people grows stronger as each year passes.

There was a two week stay in Stanley before the return journey to Montevideo, to be followed by a three week cruise on the *RMS Highland Brigade* back to England, with six ports of call on the way, it was in marked contrast to the outward journey. Like many of the experiences encountered, I had no plans to repeat them but there were few that I was prepared to regret.